OCCASIONS

Dorothy Hammond Innes

Drawings by
Cavendish Morton

COLLINS/FONTANA

First published in Great Britain by Michael Joseph Ltd 1972
First issued in Fontana Books 1974

© 1972 by Dorothy Hammond Innes

Made and printed in Great Britain by
William Collins Sons & Co Ltd Glasgow

For
RALPH
who took me to all these places,
and for my mother who travelled
more bravely than I.
Also my father's mother who
travelled more wildly still.

CONTENTS

Introduction   7
Hospitalities   9

PART I

Chablis at Home   15
Châteauneuf du Pape   19
Dordogne in Winter   23
A Dinner Not Eaten   30
Twelve Difas   35
Eating Through Rhodes   48

For Sale — Welsh Mountain Mare,
    Believed in Foal?   53

PART II

Eating Armenian   56
Cowboys for Breakfast   57
Christmas in Tenochtitlan   63
Pisco Sour   74
Chica and the Rites of Spring   81

Groaning With Strange Meats   87

PART III

The Opal-Coloured Land   93
    (We Eat Australian)

The Other Side of the Menu   124

PART IV: SAILING

Introduction   126
Rude to Be So Late   128
Eating Ashore   134
Mary Deare's Galley   147

INTRODUCTION

This is not a book about food but about occasions. Years later, I may or may not remember what we ate, but I will remember the look and feel and mood of that table. A meal gives you an excuse to stop, sit down, and look around. I observe better with a glass in my hand, almost irrespective of what's in it; a drink provides an anchor, you can't be hurried on or interrupted until it's finished. At least, you shouldn't be.

Menus I have collected as souvenirs, sometimes asked for, but sometimes, I must admit, stolen and smuggled into my handbag. Where the translations are curious, they are not printed in derision, but with gratitude that they tried to tell us in our own language what there was to eat.

Some of the most memorable meals had no menus. I have no bits of paper to remind me of the trout they caught in the lake and cooked in sour cream at the climbers' hut in Norway when they saw us coming round the next mountain. Or of the uniquely exquisite skewers the little boy grilled – on Sunday nights only – at the village of Vathahort when we sailed to the Greek island of Meganisi. Or of the fourteen courses carried by fourteen men with which the Pasha of Marrakech welcomed us to his white castle in the Atlas Mountains.

Each of these memories is tacked, sometimes lightly, to a table. But the fun is really what you see from there. So I will not wish you 'Bon appetit' but 'Bon voyage'.

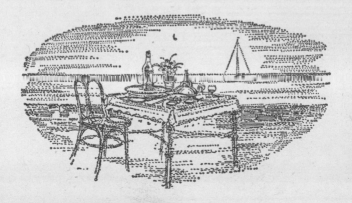

Food offered by strangers, unexpectedly, in a strange country. These moments of true hospitality leave photographs on the mind quite separate from anything before or after, each complete in itself, with the little shock of surprise when the stranger suddenly becomes a friend.

We were sitting in a train going down from Tangier to Morocco. An elegant Arab gentleman wearing a djellaba of very fine gabardine, and travelling with his secretary, suddenly leant forward and held out a beautifully manicured hand, full of almonds and raisins, first to Ralph then to me, before starting on this frugal lunch himself. The traditions of the desert, still honoured in a train.

On the Dalmatian coast, we had wandered along the cliffs from Split one evening and were trying to find a short cut back, when a tall elderly peasant woman blocked our path. Ralph produced that remembered soldier's Italian which has so often helped us in the Balkans, and explained we were seeking a way back to the town.

'*Italiano?*' she asked.

'*No, Inglesi.*'

'Ah! *Inglesi!*' she cried, and flung out both arms in a great gesture to embrace us.

There was no way through, she explained, we should have to turn back. But sit down, sit down. Opposite the cottage she had emerged from, there was a flat bit of stone wall under a big ilex tree. With gestures she delayed me from sitting, went into her home and brought back a piece of white embroidery which she spread on the rock for me to sit on (I who will sit anywhere!).

She gave us handfuls of pecan nuts and brought out a packet of biscuits, and as we ate them we talked – in a little Italian, in names, in anything, in nothing, while the dusk grew. We must wait till her niece came back from work. Her niece spoke English, she was a teacher.

Our hostess was gaunt and strong and brown like a tree. The dusk smelt of pines. She apologized for not asking us in, but it was dark indoors, she had only a candle. Can a hovel be a proud and pleasant place? In the country, away from towns, yes.

Her niece came walking quietly through the streets, like the girl in Hans Andersen who heard the nightingale sing. She was a pretty girl in a cotton dress and a beige coat. Yes, her English was excellent. She had worked hard at her English because she so much wanted to be able to read Shakespeare in the original.

We still write to her.

Sailing away from Greece and back to Malta one year, we closed Cape Matapan at night by the great swinging beam of its lighthouse, then ghosted in by starlight and our own spotlight to the little cove of Asomato just under the Cape. Terrifying to see, when daylight came, those jagged rocks so near!

As there was a most unseasonable westerly blowing, we decided to stay there for the day, so we went ashore and walked out to the headland. As we followed the little track past the lighthouse, one of the two lighthouse keepers came out to greet us. By signs he invited us all (we were five) to come in and see over his splendid lantern. We circled up the narrow stairs and he showed us proudly the details of its working. It was strange to stand actually beside that famous beacon whose finger stretches so far, and think of all the ships who make their way round this corner of Europe with their eyes on Matapan.

Downstairs again, when we tried to say goodbye, he gestured us most insistently into the living room, a large bare wooden room, its window looking landward. Here were his wife and the other lighthouse keeper. They invited us most warmly to eat with them, and pointed out that the table was already laid for us – knife, fork, bread, glass. She served a delicious mixed fish stew from a pot on the stove, the sort of stew cooked all round the fishing coasts of the world, Bouillebaisse is the version that has become famous. The bread was a little stale, it was a long bicycle ride into the village to fetch it, but it was fine for swabbing up the lovely broth. We drank a rough red wine drawn from a cask by the door served in an earthenware jug.

I wanted to return this generous friendliness, and thinking

Mary Deare might be as much fun to them as their lighthouse was to us, we asked them on board for drinks that evening.

We hardly dared hope they'd come, but at the appointed time the man and his wife appeared on shore – the other of course had to remain to man the lighthouse. One of our crew rowed ashore to fetch them, and a slight problem arose. Accustomed to the solid wooden fishing boats which you can hardly unbalance, they were nervous of our feather-light de Souto dinghy. We thought the girl was pregnant, but it was difficult to tell under all those clothes. The difficult moment was getting her up on board from the dinghy; she quickly realized that if she put her foot anywhere but in the centre it threatened to capsize, but didn't quite know what to do about it. She was fairly solid and there was quite a slop on the water. However, she was carefully manoeuvred and manhandled up on deck, and while her husband was shown the

sailing practicalities, chart table, navigational aids, etc., I gave
her the grand tour of the living quarters, which she delighted
in as a sort of super dolls' house, crooning over the cooker,
deep sink and taps and storage lockers.

Sitting over our drinks, we found so much in common, we
realized again what an international language a boat is. As the
wind was still quite fresh when they left, I tied one of my
scarves over her head in a colour I thought suited her, as a
little souvenir of us.

The next morning early, when we sailed out, beating into
the tail of the westerly, they were all up on the lantern platform to wave us off, and they even switched on the light in
salute, swinging the great white swathe out over the troubled
grey water.

A year later we passed that way again, on the reverse course,
sailing out from Malta to Greece, and as we approached Cape
Matapan we sounded our foghorn. We are very recognizable
with our simple sail plan and big ventilators, and lighthouse
keepers have sharp eyes – anyhow, not so many sailing yachts
pass that way. In a few minutes we recognized through
binoculars our three friends running up to the lantern platform. She had brought a sheet to wave in greeting as we went
by. We were proud that *Mary Deare* was a known friend to
Matapan.

Walking on the Greek island of Levkas, we left our anchorage

of Vasiliko behind and followed a road up out of the village through orchards. Two men, one old, one young, were having the sort of fierce-sounding conversation which so often makes Greek exchanges sound like the build-up to a fight. They both looked rather villainous, we thought, standing arguing in the middle of the dusty road, so far from anywhere. .

When we returned from our walk an hour or so later, we found the younger man still at the same place, waiting for us. He indicated a track leading off the road, and asked us to come with him . . . in English. We had no idea where or to what we were going, but it seemed rude to refuse as he was so pressing; besides, we were intrigued. Ralph and I had three friends with us, our crew at the moment. As he had addressed us in English, we tried to talk to him as we walked, but got no answer. We each tried in turn, in case he found certain intonations difficult. Nothing seemed to get through, no response at all, only at last a slightly puzzled, worried shaking of the head. He was obviously not deaf. What, then? The track led down through fields and fruit trees to a little farm. He waved us on. As we approached a shed, the older man came round the corner with a gun.

As so often in Greece, it all resolved into smiles and reason. They were father and son. The son owned the farm but lived in Vasiliko, and his father ran the farm for him. He lowered the gun in some embarrassment, he was only bringing it in to clean it.

We sat on a fallen tree in dappled sun and shade while his son pressed loquats upon us, golden, straight from the tree, warm from the sun, dripping with juice. As we licked the juice from our fingers and he picked more loquats for us (and picked a basketful of ripe oranges and lemons for us to take back on board) he talked to us in slow, careful, excellent English. He had learned from books. He could not – could not – understand when he heard it spoken. He walked back to Vasiliko with us, and on the way we all tried to converse with him, tried thoughtfully, making every effort. No understanding. In his house at Vasiliko he introduced us to his wife, her sister, his mother, and two daughters, and gave us wine he had made himself. He showed us his English books, chiefly that very excellent series put out by NATO. He had worked alone, no lessons, no teacher. He had longed and hoped for someone to talk English to. Now we had come, and we could not make him understand.

CHABLIS AT HOME

Chablis used to be one of the most perfect small medieval towns in France, until damaged by bombing during the last war. The Hotel de l'Etoile was famous for the cooking of the late M. Charles Bergerand. It is now owned by his nephew.

We drove down into Chablis on an early spring evening. It was as quiet and empty as any little country town seems when the men have not yet come home from work and the women are cooking.

The hotel is on a corner in the centre of the town. The door was open, and we went into a narrow, bare, dark-brown hall, with an office on the left but no one about. Then a young man with a round and smiling face emerged from somewhere – our Patron, M. Bergerand, and close behind, his mother also came to welcome us. She showed me with pride a framed certificate on the wall. It was from the Waldorf Astoria in New York, and stated that recipes from l'Hotel de l'Etoile at Chablis had been included in their series 'Dishes of Regional France'.

An alien picture swamped my mind, of the huge brilliant crowded Wedgwood Room in the Waldorf Astoria – all those waiters in hunting pink hurrying about against the pale blue walls, the menus too big to hold up, a woman at the next table stubbing out her half-smoked cigarette in the middle of the half-eaten steak that overflowed her plate – and I found myself turning Madame away from the certificate, and pouring out to her that it was not for her to be proud of that, but for

15

the Waldorf Astoria to be proud that she had given them her recipes. It was difficult to make her understand why I minded, why it mattered. I was so afraid she would think I was just flattering her.

We fetched our bags from the car and the Patron took us up the narrow stairs covered in worn linoleum and gave us the best room, the one at the corner that had its own bathroom – in a separate cubicle behind white net curtains, and hot water does come, though slowly. But why hurry? The lavatory was opposite, and had such an interesting 'Avis' on the door – differentiating most lucidly between the behaviour expected of ladies and gentlemen, also explaining the treatment preferred by the cistern – that I regret not having copied it out.

We wanted to catch the last of the chill March sunshine and drove up out of the town to the open country, and from the top of a gentle rise we saw seven – seven, seven! – three-horse teams ploughing. Beside each team of three great horses walked a man in blue, breaking for another season the rich earth of Burgundy. The rolling landscape was patched with coverts of trees, with vineyards (the vines pruned down to little black stumps), and the turned earth behind the ploughs was red in the slanting light. But the trees had that fluffy look that shows the leaves are almost ready to break.

Dusk came quickly and the teams went home. The whole earth seemed to breathe with life. Going back to the town, to go indoors, was not like leaving empty country, vanishing into the dark. It was like leaving a person.

The dining room was very plain and bare, but vibrated with that eager air of something important about to happen. Two other tables were occupied, one by commercial travellers, the other by two local men. Sad how few women are fed in public in places where the food is good.

We ate – of course – Sole cooked in Chablis. Followed by Ham cooked in Chablis, then their own Soufflé à l'Orange, which means that a whole hot orange is put in front of you, and from one section, which has been removed, there billows out the advance guard of the delectable soufflé with which the fruit has miraculously been filled. I have the recipe here beside me, but I will not read it, I prefer just to remember. They are generous with their recipes, they give them to you on little coloured cards – as well they may! All that is needed is genius. Any fool can cook a bit of sole or ham in white wine, but to carry out the Bergerand recipes and achieve the same result . . . that is Cooking.

They offer other dishes, but we have never been strong-minded enough to break away from that classic meal to try the others – besides, why come to Chablis to eat what you can eat elsewhere?

This was the night we first realized that most of the wine labelled Chablis has never seen the place. 'My vineyard is not facing full south,' said our Patron with a proud-modest smile, 'but it is on the curve of the hill, just next to the full-facing slope.' He kindly sold us half-a-dozen bottles to take home. 'I regret that I cannot let you have more, but my vineyard, alas, is not large. I need it all for the restaurant.' That Chablis, which had never left home, which had just crossed the road to his cellar . . . But ours, carefully brought home and rested, tasted almost the same, or we thought it did.

After dinner we walked in the town. Chablis already slept. How early people go to bed in France! We seem to have been the only people abroad in nearly every little country town in France. And never a dog! The interesting dog population of France, all those cross-bred personalities so noticeable in the mornings when the town is coming to life, and they circle the Place to visit their neighbours then return to take up their regular positions, each with absolute assurance in front of his own shop or house – they have all found somewhere to sleep. Only the cats dart or drift like shadows, or occasionally conduct stiff and formal ballets, two, or three, or four – leaping or swaying, fluffing or slinking, the town their own for the dark hours.

Grey stone houses, grey shutters mainly closed, shining grey cobbles, and the river glinting and disappearing, glinting and disappearing under its bridges, through the town, and a shimmer in the sky where a young moon is rising behind thin cloud. And all round the great swelling countryside breathing, moving with life. The Province of Burgundy over which the statue of Vercingetorex looks down from the top of his tremendous column, standing with his back towards Rome where he was led in chains; and round his feet in French and Latin, the words Julius Caesar said of the Gauls, 'This people, if ever they could unite, might stand against the world.'

The hotel door was locked and the young Patron came in his dressing gown to let us in, laughing aside our apologies – No, he was not in bed. No! we had not disturbed him, he was not tired – just relaxing over a digestif . . . would we not join him?

Why do we so often arrive in the rain? I suppose because we like to see places with only the people who live there, and this means taking a chance on out-of-the-season weather. (I hear it is possible to have both crowds and bad weather.)

The vines were pruned down to little black sticks, and the town square was empty and gleaming wet. Of the two chief Auberges we chose Mère Germaine because the name was familiar.

I remember us humping our suitcases up a lot of uncarpeted stairs, to a small bedroom with one of those flat, thin beds that look cold even if they're not. We went down as quickly as possible to the main room – bar, salon, dining room, everything. It was very large, with a lot of glass, but it was hot, and bright green pot plants and creepers made a false spring against the grey outside. Madame, assisted by Monsieur, was serving drinks and chatting with a few men sitting near the bar which ran almost the length of the room. We discussed the late spring, and its probable effect on the vine harvest (the Bouches du Rhône had frozen, and the maquis was burnt brown by frost). They asked us about the roads, and the conditions in the Côte d'Or, implying it was a remote foreign country in the far North.

Then we were installed at our table, the only table to be laid that night, and the little dishes began to arrive, all those little dishes which are the special delight of Provence – eggs and anchovies and tomatoes and celeri-rave and brandade and saucisson and crudités and aioli. The distinctive olive oil of Provence, the herbs. I ate Tapénade for the first time that night, squashed down into little flat pots and smoothed off like butter. Madame explained it to me; *le thon, les anchois, les olives noires, l'huile d'olive, un goût de cognac, un tout petit peu de citron – et les tapenos, naturellement!* (capers in Provencal). No, she didn't find a pestle and mortar slow – it leaves more character than the electric mixer.

We always drink the local wine wherever we are, and so one arrives sometimes at these royal occasions. She advised us on the year.

Then she came towards us with the beautiful bottle on a tin tray with two balloon brandy glasses beside it. Here, out of all the world, here! in its own home, with the rows and rows of precious dormant bushes stretching away outside in the damp dusk. Madame poured some into the brandy glasses and it steamed. Not chambré – hot. *'C'est mieux comme ça,'* she said as though it were the most natural thing in the world. *'Sentez, sentez!'* For a moment she leant with her hands on the table, smiling at us, inhaling it herself. *'Sentez! C'est bon, n'est-ce pas? – vraiment, le soleil!'* We breathed the summer, and the heavy, full-bodied drowsy southern wine slowly permeated us, saturated us.

Later, after dinner, after coffee, I noticed a large book with metal clasps, rather like a family Bible, lying by itself on a little table. I guessed it was the Visitors' Book of the house, and went across to look at it, wondering how far back it went. Flicking through the pages of holiday visitors, it seemed to have been wrenched open at a certain place, and lay flat. Both pages scrawled over with many names, crowded pages written everywhere; no addresses, just Army Unit details. And comments, messages, words, often deeply underlined. And the date, again and again, everywhere.

The spring of 1940. The French Army, broken and leaderless and utterly astonished, scattering back over their own country which no longer belonged to them, not knowing what had happened, not knowing where to go.

'Pas encore le fin.' 'Nous reviendrons.' 'Eh, quand même.' 'Pas terminé.' 'A nous la victoire – un jour ou l'autre.' 'Nous ne sommes pas vaincus.' 'Jamais les allemands . . .' 'Vive la France.' 'Vive la Patrie.' 'Eh, maintenant?' 'Au revoir la liberté, pas adieu.'

They must have stopped here, a confusion of many Units, eaten, rested, drunk the beautiful wine, moved on. It was May, the vines would be already high, the tendrils climbing almost while you looked at them. Who were they, where did they go,

what happened to them? These men whose anger and resolve jumped out of the pages. So many names, comments scrawled violently as though they were scratching their anger and their names, their names! – affirming their continued existence on stone, on history.

There was something naked and private about these pages. If anyone had come in I would instinctively have shut the book to hide them. Over the years they glowed incandescently. But the big bare room with the fringe of green and the aroma of wine was empty except for ourselves.

I had been in Brussels the spring the war ended, and saw the column of French prisoners returning from Germany, marching (the occasional shuffle to correct the step), down the Boulevard Adolphe Max from the Gare du Nord, where they had arrived, to the Gare du Midi, from which they would return to France. The skin of prisoners goes the same colour as those awful prison clothes they wear, like grey-striped-on-grey pyjamas, and many held in their hands the radiant yellow daffodils and mimosa that the Brussels townspeople lining the streets, silent, sympathetic, often in tears, thrust at them as they passed. So long out of the world, only a few dared to glance from side to side. Dust-coloured, holding the brilliant flowers, looking at nothing, they shuffled on endlessly until they were told to stop. All one day they passed, the just-living; Frenchmen returning to France.

I remembered Saint-Exupéry's bitter words: '*I was later to hear foreigners reproach France with the few bridges that*

*were not blown up, the handful of villages we did not burn,
the men who failed to die.'*

Had any of these men whose names I deciphered in Mère
Germaine's Visitors' Book been in that column of prisoners,
I wondered? Had any of them come back to Châteauneuf du
Pape years later, and turned back the pages to find this place
in the book?

The next morning in pale sunshine we were taken over one
of the vineyards by M. Philip, the son of the family who own
it – the same family to whom the land had been given so long
ago by the Pope at Avignon.

'We spent last night at Mère Germaine,' we told him.
'Naturally we drank your wine! Madame served it hot, in
brandy glasses. This was new to us . . .' He smiled. 'Did you
not like it? The Auberge belongs to us, that is how we think
it is best served. I know that generally it is served much the
same as Burgundy, chambré, in goblets. But it is a different
wine. We are far south here. Our sun is much hotter. In the
Côte d'Or at a certain stage of growth, they sometimes send
boys along the lines of the vines to pick off leaves to get more
sun to the grapes. Here, we may send boys along the lines to
arrange leaves over the bunches of grapes to screen them!
Ours is a wine of the hot sun – so we like it best served as
they gave it to you last night. Did you not like it that way?'

Above all, I remember following the farmer's lantern through the snowy woods, then going down at last into a great cavern which struck warm, and the smooth curving roof was dotted with black petals which were the folded wings of sleeping bats. They were so deep in hibernation that even lantern light swung up to show them scarcely caused a movement.

Our object in going to the Dordogne for Christmas was to visit the prehistoric caves in connection with LEVKAS MAN – including Lascaux, which we were grateful to have opened for us during the long period when it was completely closed. But there was much rain and réveillons and goose fat to work through first.

It rained for four days as we drove from Le Havre to Sarlat, and we celebrated Christmas Eve noisily and splashily there. We chose Sarlat because the guide book said (incorrectly as it turned out) that none of the recommended hotels at Les Eyzies were open for Christmas.

Our adequate but rather grim bedroom looked over the street, and the town loudspeaker opposite played joyously. Below, at the desk in the narrow busy entrance, sat a regal example of the Madames without which no small French hotel is quite right; black hair, dark eyes, black dress stiffly encasing her fine Edwardian figure; ear-rings, of course, and rings on the hands from which the ledgers grew. An unchallenged queen of her realm.

We foolishly ate dinner on Christmas Eve, as we happened to be hungry at the usual time, instead of waiting for later delights, then we walked a little way across the steep cobbled medieval city, running with water, to the Cathedral. It already seemed full, but we inserted ourselves fairly centrally towards the back, and indeed people continued to pour in during the two-hour service. A little fair girl of about four occupied three chairs in front of me, lying full length, sleeping peacefully throughout, so I had a good view of the officiating priest, leading and inspiring the exciting singing and the loud organ. Just as the supreme moment of the Mass was imminent, a man pushed his way urgently through the crowded church.

23

I think he had already been celebrating elsewhere, and was not quite sure which way to face, but he was determined not to miss his Christmas Mass.

Exhausted by noise and emotion and the crowd, we went home – still raining – and after a quiet drink went to bed. This was a grave error of judgment. The réveillon was fairly quiet, as there was much serious eating going on.

Gratinée de Fromage
Huitres
Médaillon de Foie Gras
Tournedos Rossini
ou
Dinde aux Marrons Truffée
Salade
Fromage
Bûche de Noël

But the apparently endless number of people attending it all left at different times, and wished each other a merry Christmas under our window. The greetings grew longer and louder and merrier as the night passed, and the partings more reluctant. Then of course the slamming of car doors and the revving up of engines in the rain and the cold before the final farewells were hailed across increasing distances. If we had only guessed how long the supper would last, we would have got up and dressed and gone down to join them in the early part of the night.

We drove about the lovely land of the three rivers, the Dordogne, the Lot and the Tarn, in sparse winter beauty. The rain stopped at last and we had Alpine weather, blue sky and sunshine and the sparkle of frost. Strolling through woods along the beautiful bank of the Vézère, warm in the winter sunshine, the dried leaves hanging in a painted stillness, we passed a large ruined stone house, almost a little castle, where a great hall facing the river, its doorway gaping, had so strong an atmosphere of malevolence that I – literally – dared not enter. What had conceivably happened there, to leave such active and horrible pressure?

We had moved to Les Eyzies, to a warm little bedroom charmingly decorated in Empire style, opulent in red and gold. I chose it, to the disappointment of the patronne, who wanted us to have a larger room (she had made them all a pleasure to be in) because the window looked straight towards the bulky rock profile below which Cro-Magnon Man had been found, and he was after all the object of our visit. As I don't like foie gras and can tire of confit d'oie, I lived on cèpes Bordelaises – the delicious *boletus edulis* of our own woods at home – cooked there in goose fat with parsley and garlic, followed by trout; rather ashamed to be so unseasonal but they cooked them beautifully. We drank red Bergerac 1964, Château Ladesvignes, and Blanc de Blanc (Caillenet).

Then the snow came, long and deep. By now we were at home in the *gisements*, the caves which showed signs of human habitation. We had explored Laugerie Haute and Laugerie Basse, Tayac, Abri de Boisson in the Gorge d'Enfer, Font de Gaume, Combarelles, Les Girouteaux, Bernifal, Cap Blanc. We lived in two worlds, the sunlit winter world, first green-gold then white, of delicate tracery against blue sky and shining rivers, of working farms; and that other world underground, the limestone galleries where prehistoric man had lived so crowded and so busily.

The Grotte de Rouffignac is about ten miles away from this tremendous grouping round Les Eyzies, and unlike them it is a sea cave from the time when the *causses*, those limestone ridges which bar this country, ran out to sea. It is huge, and was damaged in the early 17th century by people who saw no particular value in all those funny scratches in the rock. Rouffignac has a tramline to take you a kilometre into the cave, which is as far as there are wall drawings, but the galleries, on two levels, extend for ten kilometres. Now the little tramcar looks desolate in winter loneliness, but a farmer, M. Plassard, who is escorting us, leaps on board and starts it. Waving his spotlight, he invades the darkness, and stirs to life the animals captive on these walls for so many millenia, in life and movement as once they were. Horses, goats, bison, rhinoceros, but chiefly mammoths. Many patches of the straight lines they call 'macaroni' which represents the hunters' weapons. They did not draw the animals singly, because they were not thinking merely of one horse or one mammoth, but of many, many – all the tribe must kill to keep themselves alive. So the outline is repeated and repeated, layer upon layer, a mass of animals.

Though the tribe is thought to have lived near the entrance, their artist-priests set out to penetrate as far into the earth as possible to make their drawings. The object was to placate

25

some Earth Goddess so that she would favour their hunting, and the nearer they could get to her the better. How tense and urgent they must have been, leaving the tribe behind and advancing towards an unknown power in the remote darkness, holding their stone lamps of animal fat, to cut into the rock face the likeness of all the creatures they knew. That they remembered vividly the shape and characteristic movements one can understand, as their lives depended on watching them. The miracle is that this was transmitted to their hands; drawing in a dim light, moving along to cover a big surface with the continuous outline of one body.

The air is sweet and the gallery warm. The little tramline has often been sunk to give visitors headroom. So those early artists had often been lying on their backs and drawing above them! Beside the tramline is a long row of hollows, like giants' hip-baths. They are the beds hollowed out by hibernating bears, who generation after generation came to winter here, then sharpened their claws on the rocks before going out, leaving these deep scratches.

Lascaux had all the glamour of the unattainable. Its opening in 1948 had interrupted the natural air currents which had preserved the colour on the walls for fifteen or twenty thousand years, and an alga crept over the paintings. It was rigidly closed, while a variety of experts worked and experimented to try and save this treasure for the world. We were excited that we had been given a permit from Paris.

As you approach through pinewoods you see an astonishing number of buildings, empty and abandoned; huts, cafés, cloakrooms, and car park signs, seats, kiosks. A reminder of the thousands who came here every day during the years it was open. Near the entrance are the living quarters of the technicians responsible for the elaborate machinery now installed in the caves to preserve the paintings from further disintegration.

Jacques Marsal was waiting for us. He examined our Pass and greeted us. He is one of the four – schoolboys in 1940 – who discovered Lascaux. His story is different from the handout. 'No,' he said, 'it was not discovered by a dog falling into a hole. The Press invented that. Dogs have too much sense to fall into holes. Everyone knew about the hole. It had been used as a rubbish dump for years. Then furze and branches were put across to prevent cows from falling in. But always there was a story about this place – a sort of tradition of treasure

buried here. So one day the four of us decided to have a look.'
He had wriggled on his back down a long narrow passage, fell
the last bit, picked himself up and switched on his torch.
And saw the walls . . .

They realized they had found something important. Boys in
the Dordogne knew about Early Man as boys in a gold-mining
area know about gold; they went and told their schoolmaster.

We entered through a series of heavy metal doors and
air-locks; stood for a minute with our shoes in a tray of
disinfectant; and saw the complication of instruments recording the work of preservation (artificially reproducing the
circulation of the air). A little clock was set to mark the time
of our entrance. A final set of doors, and we saw in the light
of Marsal's torch what he had been the first person to see
when he fell and scrambled down here. Compared to the other
caves Lascaux is small and intimate. The colour is what makes
it unique; the reds and browns and yellows, ochre colours;
the colours of meat. And the consistency of fear, panic, dying
– never dead, always the last throes. The thrown back heads
of the swimming deer, the rigid groping legs of the horse
driven over a precipice, the pattern of spears and traps.
Lascaux is given a much later date than the other caves.
The genius of the work is breathtaking. They jump off the
walls at you with such desperate life, all these creatures in the
moment before death. Why is it a slaughter-house in a way
the other caves are not? It isn't only the colour, it is the
muscular contraction of the bodies, the vivid expressiveness
of every attitude, meticulously recorded from much observa-
tion. They are familiar and unchanged – horses, deer, cattle.
One is glad to escape from this vibrant charnelhouse, out
through all the airtight doors, noting the change in temperature
recorded even by three people breathing there for half an hour,
to the bare woods and the débris of a tourist mecca. Beautiful
but hellish.

But La Mouthe is our love, and best remembered. The
oldest of them all, the engravings here are set at sixty to
eighty thousand years ago, making Lascaux rather modern.

Still privately owned, it was discovered in 1895 because the
grandfather of the present owner wanted to enlarge his *cave*
to hold more wine. Its discovery led to the search for other
limestone caves with prehistoric wall paintings.

Madame Lapeyre is the present owner. She prefers to be
known as Marie. She is secretive about the ownership – might

27

not some wicked foreigner try to buy it? Certainly the Government would, if, for instance, she were not always immediately available to show it to visitors at the height of the season, when there are still the cows to be milked and the pigs to be fed. Her son is not interested in the cave; from the farming point of view it is a nuisance, bringing too many people and wasting time.

But Marie loves the cave deeply, feels herself a part of it, and shows it as a hostess. We went in a grey snowy morning, through pruned vineyards and pale fields of maize stubble to the stone farmhouse among the oak trees of Perigord Noir. She was out feeding her animals. By the memories of the people in the neighbourhood who have known her all their lives, she must be well over sixty-five, some said seventy. But her figure is trim in the neat black clothes, her movements dainty and precise, her face framed in a scarf is warm and sparkling. With her acetylene lamp she leads us past the ruins of the medieval farmhouse to the walled-up mouth of the cave. She inserts a huge key in the lock of a wooden door and we enter an airy storeroom where vegetables are laid out in rows. Carrots and gourds and apples and maize glow in the lantern light, and its small yellow flame shining up into her brown face dramatizes it back to the lines of beauty it must have had when she was young. There is an air of conspiratorial excitement about her – she might never have done this before.

She had worked with the great Abbé Breuil on the excavation of the cave when she was a girl, and had known him for fifty years, and she raised the lantern to show us with special care the groups of figures on the walls which he had made sketches of, and thus made familiar to the world; curious, composite, almost impressionist groups, each head and body so individual and alive. She explained to us how much better it is to see the cave drawings by the light of a lamp, because that was the light by which they had been drawn, and not by electricity, an amenity installed in some of the other caves. She moved as quickly and lithely as a girl; it was I who hesitated and almost tripped on the rough and sometimes slippery floor, difficult to see in the changing shadows of the lantern.

This was her cave, perhaps the most important thing in her life. She liked to spend time in it; often came here alone. I asked her if she ever found the atmosphere hostile or frightening. 'Non, madame,' she answered promptly and firmly. '*Je le trouve émouvant que nos ancêtres étaient des artistes. Très émouvant.*'

I hope I shall someday, somewhere, meet again the redoubtable little man who was once Head Waiter at the Mamounia in Marrakech. I learned so much from him, I should like to thank him. He gave me confidence – in any restaurant in the world.

We were living in the Kasbah that winter, close by the great wall of the city, looking down over a chessboard of court-yards and purple lumps of bougainvillaea to the sugar-icing line of the Atlas mountains. When the Arab world became too oppressive, we used to go outside the Great Wall, and walk along the dusty road that circled it, where the laden caravans of donkeys and mules and camels brought the country produce to Marrakech, and then duck back through a little gate into the Mamounia garden. It was meant only for gardeners and wheelbarrows, but it was a marvellous short cut for us. Men working in the gardens spraying water – actually spraying water – looked up, puzzled, but no one challenged us. Indeed, how could they? We were bona fide customers going to the hotel for a drink. Could the different world we came from actually show? – did knowledge of the rue de Kasbah look out of our eyes? Once inside the Mamounia, to have come from outside was in itself to be inferior. My clothes were all right, but I never could get there without my shoes being dusty. We used to sit on the terrace, and have our drink looking up through the oranges on the trees to the blue sky, warm in the sheltered sunshine. The denizens of this well-insulated island were South American, French, American – no English at that time. Once or twice we had lunch there. Then we decided to book a table for New Year's Eve. This was the greatest Gala of the year. People flew from South America, let alone Paris, just for New Year's Eve at the Mamounia. It was said to be more difficult to get into the Mamounia for New Year than to get into heaven. We didn't need to get in, we had our room and our roof garden in the Kasbah – we just wanted a table. We booked it, well in advance, from the Head Waiter, £10 each. 'This is not for the dinner, you understand? – just the deposit for the reservation.' There was a glint of humour in his eye – had he been poor once? He was a small man, with the indeterminate colouring and buttoned-up, busy air of a Swiss, very neat and economic in every movement. Yes, we understood perfectly.

But before the time came, Ralph was down with amoebic dysentery. Also there was an electricity breakdown in the Kasbah, and being then Christmas and a holiday, it was slow to be repaired, so I was measuring out medicine by candle-light, standing by the smelly but blessed old Valor Perfection oil stove and its life-saving warmth. I lived, indoors and out, in my beautiful pale grey Linton tweed coat, in the stony coldness of a house built for heat – shuddering with cold in long hours fighting with the telephone. 'You must put them off, but don't lose it. I want to go there, I must see that – tie them down to another date . . .' Desperately ill and furious with frustration, my husband's eyes demanded incessantly what I had done, what I was doing about it, whether the plans so hardly achieved were safely laid on for another date? I hate the telephone even in my own country, it is worse in French, and worse still with Arabs speaking French, because though they speak with great fluency, it sounds different, and the names of both people and places are difficult. 'And get that money back from the Mamounia, we can't afford to throw twenty pounds down the drain.'

A young French doctor – 'I've come to Morocco to study diseases that have become obsolete everywhere else!' – drove me round to find a chemist open to make up his prescriptions. They were shut because it was a holiday. 'We have made a law that there must always be one open for urgent calls. There is a rota. Of course, they don't keep the rota. It is one thing to make a law . . .' We found one open in the end, and then he drove me back. Did he guess I feared to run the gamut of the rue de Kasbah by myself? He knew all about l'amoebe – the dreaded, usually incurable occupational disease of Europeans working in North Africa. He had a very strong new drug, which was said to cure the amoeba but destroy the liver. 'In a couple of days I hope your husband will be easier. Then in a few days – you have a roof garden? – get him up there to lie in the sun but out of the wind. I cannot say when he can make engagements, perhaps the end of next week.'

'Have we got that money back from the Mamounia?'

For some reason I hadn't the nerve to go outside the wall and in through the gardens by myself, so I went the long way

31

round. There was nothing to fear in the rue de Kasbah – women are safe enough in a city where the young men kiss each other on meeting, and go off happily together with their fingers linked. But when *I* had been indoors for a couple of days with a cold, Ralph found it more peaceful to carry a parcel when he went out – a big rather untidy one like laundry. This establishes you as a resident and you are not bothered. Yet I always found the rue de Kasbah an ordeal. The narrow street (no footpaths, a drain down the middle) was so congested, so chaotic, with the creamy djellabas pushing and hurrying in all directions, the patient enduring donkeys picking their way endlessly on tiny feet, women sitting on the ground selling bread – outside the latrines was the best pitch – waiting till the last loaf was sold, even if it was after dark. The little square shops all open-fronted, with the proprietor sitting cross-legged in the middle like a spider in his web; in one a glow of oranges and grapefruit in huge pyramids, one full of plastics, one of materials, a terrible one full of dripping skeins of unspeakable bits of meat. Horse cabs with the whip always rising and falling, cars blaring their superiority and forcing us all, people and laden donkeys, into the shops on either side.

Next a quiet street, stacked with faggots, on one side the high white wall of the Glaoui's town palace (lots of ladies buried in the gardens, they said) with greenery cascading over it. Ah, the space and peace and coolness! – that is wealth, here. But the other side of this street is where the blacksmiths work, shoeing the donkeys and mules and horses. They put long wooden pincers on the noses of the animals to keep their mouths shut, but you see the whites of their eyes rolling as the worn hooves are attacked again – harsh shouts, and the occasional startling clatter of hooves. They tether them by sticking one hind leg up into the harness, so it is dead and cramped if left long.

I take a tram from the Jenna el Fnaa. This is the famous square all the tourists are shown. Don't these dam' touting guides know me yet? – I live here. The tram runs from the Arab-Berber city to the French city, and halfway between sit the three hotels, La Mamounia, the Miramar, and the Katoubia, resting in their sanitary belt of trees, safely insulated from both cities.

I walk up from the gate to the huge doors above their film-set steps. One shouldn't arrive like this, of course – one drives up to the Mamounia. In the hall – entrance? lounge? vestibule? – acres of carpet, islands of armchairs, little groups were arranging trips with official guides, very grand ones, with Mamounia on their armbands, who always pushed hardest in a crowd, to protect their valuable clients. I heard laborious French spoken like English – well! their shoes are shinier than mine, but at least I can talk French which doesn't hurt the ears of Frenchmen. One must have something to boast about.

The usual great dining room is sealed today, but people are already lunching in another room. A waiter greets me and asks if I want a table. I explain that I want a word with the Head Waiter. He smiles pleasantly, 'Well, I am a Headwaiter, madame, but I know who you mean. He is not at lunch today, because he is supervising the final decorations for tonight, but I will tell him.' As he went, he waved aside another waiter, 'Madame does not want a table, she is not lunching today. She wants to speak to M. X.' So I was protected. There were several Headwaiters, who were tall and young and handsome, but when M. X. came everyone fell away as before a king. He came at once, walking quickly, but with no air of impatience. I explained that we had a reservation for tonight (I produced the piece of paper), but that my husband had l'amoebe (second piece of paper, doctor's prescriptions, in case he didn't believe me). He took it and read it, perhaps to see what doctor we had found, where we were living, wondering a little about us? I realized I needn't have brought it, he was a man who would make up his own mind whether people were telling him the truth. But first he said, 'Bring a chair for Madame.' They went down the steps and brought one up from the dining room. So I sat in state, and saw my shoes. He bowed. He regretted very much my husband's illness, it was not good, l'amoebe. It was disappointing about tonight. He would return my deposit. He went to a till which seemed to put the notes into his hand before he touched it. He hoped to see us both again when my husband had recovered.

He could not have been away from his decorations for more than five minutes (I had a fleeting, longing thought of the vast main dining room with slaves crawling all over it arranging exquisite fantasies), but his manner could not have been different for visiting queens. I was an unknown foreign woman with dusty shoes, interrupting the busiest day of his year to ask for my money back. He had shown me, once and for all, how a great Head Waiter behaves – not for my sake, but for his own standard. For the rest of my life, I should know that if any waiter, anywhere, treated me with less courtesy, it was he who had failed, not I.

I fear we set up an all-time record by eating twelve *difas* in a fortnight. We had the good fortune to be south of the Atlas at the time of the annual tax-gathering, and each kasbah celebrated the end of this event with a *difa*, or feast. As we were guests of the French *Officiers des Affaires Indigènes*, and as each attended the tax collection in his region (to see too much money didn't find its way into the tax-collector's own pocket) he was invited by the Caid to his *difa*, and took us along with him.

This was during the last months of the French Protectorate in Morocco, and was the first long colourful journey Ralph and I made together.

I remember the look of the country even before I remember the *difas*. Brown desert country except for the great swathe of green in the Draa valley, and sometimes in a village the dark pink of almond blossom and the bare white twigs of fig trees looking from a distance like blossom. 'Kasbah country'. The kasbahs are built of mud bricks – you can see them laid out to bake in the sun when new ones are being made.

The word kasbah is sometimes used for a single building and sometimes for a whole district in a town; it means a fortified – defensible – place. Here in the south of Morocco I remember the kasbahs as great straggling brown buildings, beautiful with their piled-up castellated roofs, and a huddle of small buildings clustered round them just like a medieval castle with its village. They are rabbit warrens, fifteen thousand people sometimes live in one. They are the colour of the surrounding sand, and when they begin to crumble they are abandoned and a new one is built as near as possible, to simplify the move. This in turn is abandoned, so that behind the kasbah now occupied, you see like a ghost over its shoulder the shell of the old one already breaking down, and beyond that again the remains of one yet older, which is only a brown mound soon to dissolve completely, back into the sand.

We ate the *difas* sitting on cushions on the floor round a central dish, in the main hall of the kasbah, eating with the right hand. Between courses water was poured into a bowl

and offered with a towel to wash our hands. These appointments varied with the wealth of each kasbah, from exquisite silver jugs and bowls and fine embroidered lawn you were ashamed to crumple by drying your hands on, to a plain bowl and a little square of cotton.

I don't know why my memory is invaded, when I remember *difas*, by the face and attitude of the Caid who was our host at one of the small kasbahs. He was an older man, who, having waited on us, withdrew and sat by himself on the floor in a corner. It was customary that he should not eat till after his guests, but we were told he was not well. Illness admitted by a Berber chief is not usually a light thing. He looked frail and his brown skin not a good colour. He must have been sitting averted from us, because I remember the angle of his head as he turned to smile charmingly and encouragingly at us between courses, gesturing us to eat well; but I think it was an effort. He had got up from his bed to be host at the *difa*.

The other guests were the chief men of his village and household, only four or five. The walls with their deep narrow windows seem high when you're sitting on the floor. A cup of goat's milk was passed round from mouth to mouth. I remember thinking (foolishly) 'If I don't catch something now, I never shall.'

The dishes at *difas* followed the same pattern, though again they varied in number and elaborateness with the different kasbahs. I learned to make my meal from the first two dishes, which I liked best, and toyed with the rest. First the Pastillia, a pigeon pie under very fine millefeuille pastry, sometimes dusted with icing sugar. Next the chickens; these are generally the little squab-sized chickens who pick about round the kasbahs, one for each person. The point is that they are cooked very slowly with olive oil and ripe lemons. The quarters of lemon are impregnated with chicken, and delicious, and the lemon juice has permeated the chicken. At the grander *difas* they are copiously sprinkled with grapes or raisins and almonds. Next the *Mechui*, a whole sheep very well roasted so that the flesh pulls easily and cleanly off the bone in neat little mouthfuls. Then *tagines* follow endlessly, all different, but composed of mutton or goat with various vegetables.

The superb quality of this food results from the cooking method. Except for the *Pastillia* and the *Mechui*, each dish is cooked in a *tagine*. These are earthenware pots, often huge, with very high lids, pointed like the traditional Welsh hats, and cooked very slowly in clay ovens. The high lid conserves and blends the *vapeur* produced by the long cooking. The thickness of the pottery also seems to have an effect. I discussed this cooking a few years later with Jeanne and Alexandre Dumaine when we stayed at his Côte d'Or at Saulieu during the period when he was the premier chef of France. As a young man he had been sent to Algiers by the French government, then still promoting North Africa. He confirmed that at its best it was superlative cooking, not easy to emulate with other cooking pots and other stoves. (Perhaps his Poulet en Vapeur, one of his most famous dishes, which you had to order two days in advance, was influenced by his knowledge of Arab cooking?)

The final course of a *difa* was *cous-cous*. Very dull, I thought, though I did learn to roll the little white grains up into a neat ball to eat it.

I have since eaten imitations of these dishes in restaurants, but even in French restaurants in North Africa, they do not compare. Partly because the cooking method is different, but also because they think it necessary to elaborate the dishes, thereby spoiling their individual character. As for *cous-cous* – it arrives trimmed up with so many garnishes! – but why bother? Perhaps people eat names? Call it pounded millet and who would want it, except in the traditional circumstance of its being a useful, easily carried food for hungry people in the desert.

Our most splendid *difa* of all was (naturally) the one given us by the Glaoui. We had had an appointment to meet him at his palace in Marrakech, and duly presented ourselves. We hardly expected to meet this legendary figure, Hadj Thami el Glaoui, The Great Caid, Pasha of Marrakech, himself; he was already 76, and seldom saw Europeans apart from old friends. We thought it would be one of his sons who would receive us – educated at the Sorbonne or in England, very Europeanized.

The gateman was expecting us, always a relief when the gate is between different worlds. We stepped from the dusty street into the green moist lovely garden full of oranges and lemons and grapefruit hanging on the trees, and brilliant flowers. We were welcomed at the door by a member of the staff in a very fine djellaba and turban who took us to a council chamber and left us. It was dim after the sunshine and smelt faintly of cedarwood from the doors. A semi-circle of leather pouffes, one side green and the other side purple, were arranged round a central pouffe.

We waited restlessly. At last he returned and indicated we should follow him. No word was spoken, we had none in common. He gave us a long and impressive tour of the state-rooms of the palace. I must have been nervous, because I retain only a general impression of settings appropriate to the Arabian Nights. I was afraid we were going to be fobbed-off with this. Also, we had heard of the dancing at the Glaoui's castle deep in the Atlas mountains and I longed to see it, and was rehearsing in my mind what I would say to him. We walked through endless great rooms, making varied noises of appreciation.

Finally we were led away, it seemed, from the main palace, through the gardens to a smaller, modern building. Our escort passed us on at the door to a still higher personage, who waved us in and in turn passed us on to a short, thickset dark man in a European suit who welcomed us in French. I didn't know who he was, but Ralph murmured it was the Glaoui's personal secretary – an Armenian – always with him. He led us into a small bare modern office – and there he was. El Glaoui. Very tall and thin as he rose to greet us from behind a little desk with a toy tank on it, in his flowing robes of immaculate, dazzling white from which his brown aquiline face emerged like the head of a distinguished turtle. The curved Berber dagger rested on his left hip.

We all sat down and though I knew he spoke perfect French and I believe some English, he liked the conversation to go through his secretary. This is something I have noticed in other men who have lived very dangerous lives; they have formed the habit of allowing themselves time to think between hearing and answering. I geared my answers to his questions to emphasize our preference for the Berber areas – which was absolutely sincere – and told him how much we were looking forward to going South, to the Atlas and beyond : his country. French is such a helpful language to pay compliments in ! In French-speaking countries I often become our spokesman, I seem to live with the prefix '*mon mari dit* . . .' on my lips.

Looking at this smiling, quiet-spoken man of great dignity, it was easy to imagine him staying at Claridge's and being received at Buckingham Palace as the ruler of his people. Harder to realize that this was the Lord of the Atlas, the one rival the Sultan feared, who had swept across Morocco with his Berber tribesmen as his fathers had done before him, though none had aimed as high as he. He had gambled on backing the French, and when we met him he was still a power, the great challenger, his future trembling.

With a smile of great charm and a wide gesture towards us, he made a long speech to his secretary which sounded like instructions. The secretary then passed on the invitation in French; to visit his castle of Telouet, have lunch there, and after, see the Berber dancing. As I began to thank him, a second speech of instructions poured out in the soft, guttural Arabic. 'El Glaoui would like you to see also a quite different style of Berber dancing at another of his castles, South of the Atlas, at Taourirt. That would be at night. All this will be arranged.'

Two years later, this old man, by then 78, was to advance to the very walls of Fez with ten thousand Berbers, and proclaim the aged Moulay Mohammed Ben Arafa as Sultan, in place of Sidi Ben Youssef, whom he himself had originally placed on the Sultan's throne. But he lost. The French had used him, they abandoned him. Ben Youssef, later to pronounce himself king, kept the Glaoui waiting all day for the audience to make his surrender, and then required him to advance the length of the great audience chamber on his knees.

Telouet lies like snow on the brown Atlas at 8,000 feet, vast, turreted, completely isolated. As we turned off the pass through the mountains and followed the road that leads only to Telouet, we felt how improbable it was that this feudal stronghold, from which the Glaoui had launched his forays into history, could conceivably be expecting us. It had only been yesterday . . . how could instructions arrive ? Yet the brown village huddled round the castle was lit by occasional splashes of white – women in their special finery, glittering with silver, moving towards the castle in twos and threes. Was there something on? Was it for us?

As we drove into the great courtyard the Glaoui's Khalifa, a most impressive major-domo, host in his master's absence, advanced to meet us.

Our own driver-interpreter always stuck to us like glue when food or cameras were around, and indeed was invaluable. (He claimed to have been Churchill's driver when he was in Marrakech . . . or do all hire-car owners claim that? He was of sufficient calibre for it to be true, a vigorous diplomat who solved many problems for us.)

The room to which the three of us were taken was fairy-like. The openwork tracery of the high plaster walls was like lace, and enchanting perspectives led off to corridors and turrets. We sat in the curved, cushioned window seat of one of the turrets – outside the window stretched the huge ramifications of the castle, and beyond it the hills still rising to the pass.

This *difa* had fourteen courses, each carried in by a different servant. At one stage the four next courses – four lordly *tagines* standing on the floor each with its bearer beside it – were waiting in line against the wall. Each dish, *Pastillia*, chickens, *Mechui*, and all the successive *tagines*, were superlatively cooked, the silver appointments and embroidery exquisite. Towards the end I became increasingly conscious of music stealing in. 'Has it started?' I asked our driver, who was always a good ADC. 'Madame, they await your pleasure,' he said.

So we went out on to a balcony above the main courtyard, and the sudden brilliance of the white castle against the blue sky was dazzling in that sunshine after the shade inside. Looking down we saw a great horseshoe of dancers, sixty-four women, in flimsy white muslin with coloured scarf-head-dresses, the lovely Berber silver jewellery massed on neck and ears and wrists. They move all the time with a flowing undulating movement of the whole body, so the semi-circle sways like a cornfield in the wind. The two women at each end of the horseshoe were the leaders, the best dancers, using ceaseless, rhythmic arm movements. In the mouth of the horseshoe sit the male musicians in a group, with a fire to keep the skin of the tam-tams taut. As we came out they broke into a song of welcome – 'To you who have come from far across the sea.'

These are not professional dancers. They are the women of the village dancing the traditional dances of the mountain

Berbers – different in each district – for the entertainment of their Caid's guests. Something feudal and unbuyable. They regard such events as a high day and holiday, and continue to wear their finery about the kasbah for several days afterwards.

'How long do they go on?' I felt I ought to ask after about an hour. I could have stayed for ever, mesmerized and enchanted. 'Madame, they will go on dancing as long as you are here.'

So it was for me to go. They brought the mint tea, always a farewell ceremony. After the third cup you leave, and the length of the pauses between the cups implies how ready or reluctant they are for your departure. They were charmingly slow, but at last we had sipped the third cup served from the beautiful tray, and must turn away from the magic continuing below.

As we left the balcony our driver said to me in a business-like way: '*Madame, vous avez besoin du water-closet?*' Startled, I collected myself in time to say 'Yes.' He called a servant whom I followed with some curiosity. What he led me to was a superlative contemporary bathroom, big enough to hold a dance in, equipped with every possible fitting, including of course a bidet, all low and streamlined, in pale jade green with silver taps. And everything worked. A bit of Paris imported by the Glaoui's son.

Ralph meanwhile had been invited to join me. After all,

I ate with him, where did we draw the line? But he thought he'd establish that we have our tribal customs too.

Ant-Atlas, Atlas Noir, the old range to the south, is to me more impressive than haut-Atlas, the high sugar-coated barrier you watch from Marrakech. Bare and covered with sharp stones which each throw a shadow, hence their name. On a night drive through the endless hairpin bends we saw a tiny glow far ahead. In every successive bend we lost it, then saw it again, each time a little bigger and brighter as we drew nearer. When a last bend brought us upon it, we saw it was a little fire of sticks in a curve of the rock wall beside the road, and two men were sitting eating their supper. It was just a glimpse of brown faces and the flash of teeth and eyes as they looked up to wave at us, and the outline of their camels tethered by them; then we were past, leaving them in the loneliness of the mountains.

South of the Atlas was still called The Zone of Insecurity. We found the local French establishment intended to accompany us to see the Glaoui's dancers the following night, as this entertainment had never been put on for them. So we led quite a troop into the dark castle of Taourirt, which was doubly mysterious to us as we had not arrived there till dusk, hadn't seen it by daylight and had no idea where we were going.

Naphtha flares illumined the dark wild faces of the men waiting to welcome us. Through a big gateway into a narrow dark mud passage, up a curving mud staircase black between the splashes of torchlight. We emerged on to a flat roof, were guided to a row of chairs, and looked down into the central courtyard.

A fire blazed, the musicians beside it were a biblical group huddled in their cloaks, and the dancers were already assembled, glimmering in their long full white muslin dresses. But around us the walls of the kasbah rose still higher, and from above us boys continuously leaned out over the walls to throw bundles of furze down into the courtyard to replenish the fire. Each time a shower of sparks flew up redly from the yellow flames, and if you tore your eyes away and looked upward, in the square of sky framed in the castellated walls a crescent moon, infinitely remote, looked very white by contrast.

The women's silver ornaments glittered as they swayed in the dance, and the clash of the tambourines rose with their

singing, that long-drawn ululation of the tongue – *Aiya!* – that emphasizes the rhythm of body and drum until it becomes a crescendo growing with its own repetition, an hypnotic compulsion, wiping out time. Every now and then one of the musicians rose from the group and held his tambourine close to the fire to tighten the skin, and great rangy dogs, like the hunting dogs of medieval tapestry, moved among the dancers, brushing their skirts.

A third *difa*, different again, was out-of-doors. On the Northern slopes of the Atlas we rode on muleback with the French Controlleur Civile. The group of mules and their Berber drivers were waiting for us at the farthest point reachable by car. My mule was pale grey and beautiful, his ears not very long, in dim light he could pass for a horse. He was very intelligent, pushed the others aside in fording a stream, and picked his way unerringly along the outside edge of the path circling the hillside (there is always a fall of stones on the inner side, from the slope above, but the outer part is nice and smooth).

As our host was making his annual tour of the remoter villages in his area, we were welcomed at each village by its Caid and offered café cannelle (coffee flavoured with cinammon) passed up to us as we sat on muleback. My saddle was covered with a gay cloth, but as the miles passed it occurred to me there was nothing else between me and the wooden saddle. Then another hour's riding and another thousand feet up, and another glass of café cannelle, and the women of the village came out to greet us with the strange cry of welcome which, in a different tone, they also use to drive the men into battle.

It was cool, with some mist. The villages were mud huts that seemed to grow from the side of the mountain. From one village the chief rode out a long way to meet us, an old man on a white mule, and he was *wearing steel-rimmed spectacles*. As he and the group escorting him were some way off, I asked the Controlleur about this startling incongruity. 'He was blind, with astigmatism in both eyes,' he explained. 'It was a tragic sight. He was in his prime then, yet always he had to be led by his sons, one on either side. Then one year, on a visit like this, I had a friend with me who was an eye specialist in Algiers. He said, "I think I could cure that man." I explained to the chief that it would mean going to Algiers, and the result could not be certain. He decided to go. What courage! – to place himself utterly in the hands of strangers. He had never been farther than Marrakech before, and to understand and accept an anaesthetic was to give others total power over him, far from his village and his tribe. He said he would go because he trusted me! I think I was more frightened than he was – how could I have faced his village again if it had gone wrong? But it was a success, and now he rides ahead as you see him, alone.'

I had given up expecting to arrive anywhere, I thought jogging along on my mule up stony tracks above a ravine between rocks of increasing bulk and wildness was my life. But suddenly there was the glow of a fire, and a river flowing out of a wall of rock, and a mass of people. Three villages had combined to give this feast, bringing all the dishes up by mule to meet at this sacred place, the *source d'eau*.

They had killed a sheep and examined the entrails, and thought the weather would be fine, but it was very cold and a faint mountain drizzle had started, turning to sleet. One of the Berbers lent me his glorious long cloak of indigo-blue wool; I wrapped myself in it and felt I could never be cold again. The tam-tams started up as we ate, I had not heard them in the open before, they creep round the mountains as bagpipes do, defying the loneliness.

On the other side of the ravine a crowd of people, the population of the three villages, sat along the edge of the cliff to watch. I have pictures like that in the illustrated Bible I had

44

as a child, of the children in the wilderness. As the sleet turned to flakes of snow, the rugs we were sitting on were moved into a cave. The music grew louder and the women danced, the fire blazed and the silver twinkled. The women were not in white here – these were poor villages – but in a varied smother of dark and vivid colours. Here for the only time we saw male dancing, very virile and acrobatic. I have only seen dancing of the same character from Russians. In a ring of women who stamped and clapped their hands and sang the rhythm, two men faced each other in the Dance of the Courting Pigeons. Every strut and flutter, advance and retreat, peck and circling, meticulously expressed through the human form.

I had forgotten my wooden saddle until I sat on it again. The jolt of going down was worse than going up. When we arrived at the appointed place for the cars to meet us, on the other side of the mountain from where we had left them, they were not there. Rain had washed the road away. So we rode on, and it grew dark. At last I had decided that I could not bear another jolt, I would dismount and *walk*, when I heard a cry of good cheer from my companions, and saw faintly ahead the misty light of headlights turned on to beacon us to the cars. Still, I was sorry to say goodbye to that mule, I would have liked to bring him home.

Men in love with a country other than their own hand a big hostage to fortune. South of the Atlas les Officiers des Affaires Indigènes administered the land, and we stayed with them. One, who with his company of the Foreign Legion had built the Pass of Tizi n' Tishka through the Atlas. Another who had mapped Fez (that labyrinth!). They were a hand-picked ten per cent of volunteers from the French Colonial regiments. They were responsible to the Sultan's Government, not to Paris – indeed, when we were in Paris we felt they were forgotten.

They knew time was running out. Not in the sense of losing your job, but in the sense of whether you got your throat cut, and the dainty young wives a few of them had got out there because they believed in this country, and the so *French!* little children jumping on and off the overcrowded Arab country buses, and running through the desert *souks*. A world that seemed to us totally unconnected with the business French of Casablanca or the political French of Rabat, very few of whom ever ventured here, or took any interest.

These hard-bitten, dedicated men, all sooner or later eaten by

l'*amoebe*, never taking time off to go back to Vichy for the cure that might, taken in time, check it, administered enormous territories and had no force of arms behind them. Two camel corps of thirty Taouregs each, patrolled from the Ant-Atlas to Lake Chad, under a junior French officer. The method was to throw the volunteer French boy to his Taouregs and see how they got on. If they liked him he could stay – nothing else would have worked.

A young, fair *sous-officier* came into Tagounit with one of the Camel Corps while we were there. This is where a sign-post in the sand says 'Timbouctou, 50j' (fifty days by camel). He was radiant after his first patrol, when he had been sent out with a map reference to meet his corps, then to ride with them, because obviously these wild Blue Men had accepted him, he was one of them, they joked together and were teaching each other. When he had set out to meet them he didn't know their language and had not ridden one of these long-legged racing camels before. (They let me mount one and ride a very little way, just for fun.) *Les Hommes Bleus* are supposed to be so-called because the indigo they dye their cloaks with rubs off on to them, but it seemed to me that their skins had a natural dark blue sheen.

We stayed two days in Tagounit while torrential rain made the *piste* impassable. We slept in a bare stone room in a little Beau Geste fort some way across the sand from where our host slept. I thought how incongruous my pot of face cream looked on the window-sill, which was really a gun-embrasure. Our morning coffee was brought to us in bed by a splendid Taoureg in a flowing blue cloak. During the day we sat over a little brushwood fire in another small fort, our host's quarters, and talked to him. Tall, dark, sardonic, in a shabby uniform with a worn-out jeep, he still, somehow, had the air of being the absolute power in that land.

Like any man whose work is his whole life, once his initial reluctance to discuss it has been worn down (reluctance because he doubts if anyone can care or understand about his work and his world) he couldn't stop. He talked in a torrent as only Frenchmen talk, the philosophy and the practice woven together. When the rain stopped we walked with him in the *souk* – it only operated once a week, on market day; everything, even firewood, had to be trucked over the Atlas by the road that he had built. 'It's a good road! – we shall get some dinner,' he said. The men in the market practically dug him in the ribs to tell him jokes and news brought with the goods from Marrakech, yet his word was unchallenged law, though he had no means to enforce it. Why? Chiefly because the endless land claims, which are the main business of an administrator in the desert where every area round a water-hole is so precious, had never before been judged impartially. Also, as with any Arab or Berber, the personal response to an individual, not to a system.

When the *piste* was passable, he drove us still farther south, to M'hamid, the last outpost. The *piste* was a just-perceptible line across the desert, nothing interrupted the rolling brown on either side. As we approached M'hamid, another small fort with a twin-towered gateway, there, amazingly, were the camel corps drawn up on either side, presenting arms. I saw it through tears.

I have spent quite a lot of time in France and French territory, but this moment, this superb, unnecessary flourish of pride in a time of disintegration, is to me all the *panache* of France.

I'm told there are very good hotels in Rhodes – outside the town. As our object was to discover the town, we never emigrated to that well-insulated reserve. When we went ashore from *Mary Deare* in search of a meal, we usually began dinner at a large, straggly, indoors-outdoors restaurant at the end of the waterfront, where the cafés and shops and lights have petered out.

Almost always we ate outside, under a cover flapping slightly in the usual cool on-shore evening breeze, the hot air over the land rising and the cooler air from the sea moving in. Always a coat at night in June.

The food was not bad – indeed, I remember the best octopus and squid I ever ate were once served there as an hors d'oeuvre, cooked and served separately, good because they were both very young and had been cooked very slowly. But we went there for the variety of entertainment to be seen from this rather draughty dining room built out over the beach. One's neck was in perpetual motion, trying to watch three spectacles at once.

On the other side of the dark curve of the bay, the Castle had Son et Lumière! We never went to see what story they were really telling – we thought it looked better from across the bay – so we made up our own story as we got to know the sequence of lighting effects. Above the dark sea the different colours flickered over the ancient stones; (the mysterious green light was when he climbed up to her window; the pale single star was the first soldier of an invading army probing for an entrance; the wild outbreak of yellow and orange was the battle, and then oh, terrible! the climax, the castle burning, the red smoky glow enveloping it).

We could never watch the Castle sequence through because of the distraction of a cabaret going on at the other end of our restaurant, music and singing, once a belly-dancer. And between these two diversions, and perhaps the best – setting out to sea for their night's fishing, the Lampari! Each mothership towing six little cockleshells like a line of ducklings astern, and on board them all, the dazzling white acetylene

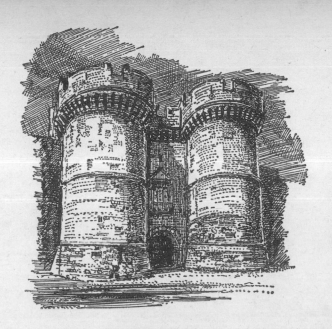

lamps to attract the fish; glaring brilliance on the black water, fading so rapidly to distant stars, then vanished, then look! look! here comes another.

The Greek reluctance to clear tables (excellent assumption of leisure!) leaves four or five people, who have all eaten different dishes, peering at each other over piles of débris. And the ghost-thin cats move like shadows over the ground, everywhere, and if you put your hand down to give something to the weakest, the thinnest, the most nervous, the little white one with only one eye, your hand goes down into a slashing savage world of the ceaseless struggle to survive. You have to time it when the waiter isn't looking, also he kicks them away when he thinks you aren't looking.

Cool on the edge of the sea, we leave and walk back to the lit café area, and stop for coffee and loukoumi. Again outside, but here there is the width of the boulevard, and another line of restaurants between us and the beach, and all the lights and people make it warmer. What a kick those tiny cups of Turkish coffee – no, no! café grec, of course – have! Though so little liquid one could take it in a mouthful if one were

49

foolish enough. And the single rich and shining square of Turkish Delight on a toothpick, and the glass of water.

On again to trees and darkness. We turn into the Street of the Knights and walk into the past. On our right the tall dignified houses still bear the coats of arms of their great original masters. (What was it? To be admitted to the Order of the Knights of St John, you must prove noble birth on both sides of the family for at least four generations.) These dedicated formidable armoured men, drawn from the great families of Europe, still loom over Rhodes where they were defeated as they do over Malta which they held.

The houses are still lived in – by who? Divided into apartments and flats, it seems, but still alive, still real, still homes. And on the other side trees drooping over the walls, and glimpses into courtyards and gardens, sudden headily fragrant clouds of jessamine and honeysuckle.

We plunged into lights and shops and people again in the steep main street of the old Turkish town. And here we made a wonderful discovery! A tiny shop which attracted us in because of the livid and deadly colours of the liqueurs displayed in the window in big chemist's bottles. We sat at the one table in the empty shop. There was a glorious smell of hot, almondy baking. Then a very small old man emerged from the back premises carrying a large baker's tray, and put it on the counter. He was followed by a very small old woman carrying another tray. On them, hot and fresh, were packed in tight rows all the best sweetmeats sold in the sweet-shops, pastry-shops, cafés and hotels of the main part of the town. This was where they came from! We had stumbled upon their source. The trays of unbelievable delights were being neatly stacked and labelled for the various vans coming to collect them. Why had we eaten any dinner? They smiled upon us, more as visitors than customers. No, they didn't make coffee (obviously they would have no time for that ceremony). They offered to fetch us some from the nearest café . . . no, no, don't trouble, but . . . are those for sale? Yes, which did we like? Little tongs came out; these? and these? and these? And a liqueur? He smiled so proudly over his absurd coloured bottles, that we each sampled a different coloured syrup – cordial – red, violet, green, orange, to sip with the hot fresh-almond petits fours, while the tiny old couple came and went, bringing out the night's baking, busy, inspired gnomes amassing the sweetmeats of the Arabian Nights.

Later we bought a red mat of Turkish workmanship in a rather dangerous shop higher up the street. The owner's son wanted to sell us a swordstick, and kept flashing the blade out and whirling it about to show us its charms. And farther on again we bought an exquisite cloth of golden-brown drawn threadwork on white.

Then the sudden transition from the street of bright little shops to the empty, dark, tree-lined roads as we wound our way down to the harbour again, to *Mary Deare* lying stern-on to the quay, the boulevard empty now, the cafés silent, their chairs and tables stacked up ready for the morning's sweeping . . . but oh! to think of all those sweets arriving at their back doors!

Lunch in Rhodes was quite different. On the way back – from our first visit to the fortifications, I think it was – we found a square with a restaurant whose menu, displayed largely on a board, so fascinated us that we automatically sat down.

CAFE BAR OF RHODES
JOHN NITTY
EVDIMOU
No. 20

SERVES THE MOST EXOTIC FOOD
SPECIALITIES ARE

STEAKS   CHICKEN   OMELET   GRILLED MEAT
BALLS AND SIZKEBAB PLUS SALAD
OF DIFFERENT STYLES

MOST SANITARY AND UNEXPENSIVE

COME ON! COME ALL!

It was a good restaurant, you walked along the line of things cooking on skewers or over charcoal braziers, and made your choice. The other side of the square was rather unsightly because of demolition. (I knew it at intervals over five years, and the half-demolished wall never changed by a single brick, though our restaurant became three, and much grander.) The square provided a certain amount of shade from the buildings, and to it came the barrow-men for their siesta. Early in lunchtime, almost with the aperitif, the first would arrive, push his barrow into the best patch of shade, climb into it and compose himself for sleep. Then another and another until every patch of shade was occupied by barrows holding their sleeping owners.

When the sun at its height imposed a painted quiet everywhere, some late straggler, finding no shade, would have to park his barrow in the sun and creep underneath it to sleep.

I must remember not to have more than one Whisky-Mac, however sharp the wind, however mud-caked my gumboots. If I have a second, as I sip it, something happens to the walls. They fail to keep the outdoors out.

In autumn we came into a bleak little pub at a cross-roads, with the usual good Welsh fire. Everything was dimly brown – that yellowish-brown, except for the sharp black and white rectangles of Sale notices on the walls. I hate Sale notices of cattle markets, they smell of fear; but sitting at the plastic-covered table in the window they are straight opposite me, and it is difficult to avoid my eyes resting on them. Store Cattle. Fat Ewes. Pigs. Then her paragraph – one line. WELSH MOUNTAIN MARE, BELIEVED IN FOAL.

The sale was on Saturday. This was only Tuesday. Where was she now? Standing on some wet hillside, tearing at the sweet rich grass, not knowing the world could ever end. So they weren't certain she was in foal? Presumably she knew. Very peaceful, with the rustle of the wind and the silent companionship of the sheep drifting past her, and her own loud tearing at the grass.

This is when the walls began to thin. I was very aware of that moist green-brown world outside, because we'd spent the day at the Brechfa Sheepdog trials, and the look of it haunted like a ballet. The black-and-white dogs looked so tiny, crouched to the ground watching the big brave handsome sheep, who stand and stamp their feet at the dogs to show they have no fear. With infinite patience the dogs, flattened, crouch and

53

watch, every muscle, every nerve, and that sharp, single-track brain, focused on the sheep, waiting, sensing, anticipating which way they will go. Then like a loosed spring the scrap of black-and-white fur moves up the hillside, not directly, but racing in an enormous arc to get on the far side of the sheep without startling them. How can something so small move so fast, so far, for so long, so often? One dog-owner had come from half across England to compete – he had had Polio, and was crippled. 'His dogs know they have to do it all, that he can't help them with the sheep like the other men do. Watch now! He does very well sometimes.' Then as the man made a wide movement with his arms, 'Look, now, he's asking her to come in,' and the wet, draggled, quicksilver bitch came towards him. All the phrases are co-operative, never dictatorial – not 'come here', but 'ask her to come in'.

'I start to train them at different times, depends when they show an interest, they are all different, you know. This one I have only been working with for six months, I am surprised she has come so far.'

The lilting voices, the sheep, the working dogs, and the great background of the wet russet grass – through how many centuries has this skill been practised in these Welsh hills? 'But it is the Scotsmen who breed these dogs, you know! Only the Scotsmen have the secret of the breed. They do say they cross them with foxes sometimes!'

A horrible column of print is in the back of my mind – farming notes in a newspaper. 'Sheep are the only stock with which modern methods have shown little progress up to now. But Mr So-and-So has conducted very profitable experiments in keeping sheep who have never seen a blade of grass, never been out of doors at all!'

Upon these dogs, these men, and this hillside lies the painful glamour of the end. I have finished the second Whisky-Mac and there are no walls to keep out the wet, green-brown world that is real, and strong, has endured so long but which is doomed. I avoid looking at the Sale poster as I go out, but I cannot forget it because it is photographed on my mind. 'One Welsh Mountain Mare, believed in foal.' Four more days till the Sale on Saturday. Where will she take it, presuming she is in foal? A Dutch meat market? A Polish mine? It's only the whisky makes me melodramatic. She may become some nice little girl's riding pony. Oh, yes? And when the little girl grows up and wants something better? Another Market.

Pure chance who buys her, who offers most money on that particular day.

She doesn't know yet, it's only Tuesday, she is fading into the dusk on her hillside, unable to imagine trucks, and towns, and crowds and noise and sticks, the terror of a sea passage. By Saturday I shall be hundreds of miles away, I shall have forgotten her. I shall not. One Welsh mountain mare for sale, believed in foal.

PART II

EATING ARMENIAN

In New York one blowsy, humid Indian Summer afternoon, we went to Greenwich Village. We'd only been there at night before, the usual tour of night spots.

Now we are visiting friends who'd got married since our last visit to the States – they'd been courting between Harvard and Vassar then, so conveniently near to each other. The young just-become-a-grandmother was delightedly wheeling the new baby in its pram back and forth round a shady corner of the almost-empty street. When we went into the house, old and not many storeys, we topped the stairs to look right through the sitting room of the flat to trees in the garden, baby clothes on a line. The room was full of cosy old furniture, and too many books for the bookcase, and a few modern paintings and bits of sculpture. A cat – our host introduced it as 'our other child' – strolled in to sit on a table in the last of the sun. We might have been in Montmartre, or Bloomsbury.

'We're taking you to dinner at an Armenian restaurant, just round the corner. You eat mutton or mutton or mutton, but it is cooked in ways that are new to us, and it's fun to see what they've done to the cellar – just a little paint and some good ideas. They're a family of Armenians who descended on that old house a few weeks ago, we don't know where they came from.'

COWBOYS FOR BREAKFAST

You wouldn't expect real cowboys to put nickels in the juke-box to hear old cowboy songs, would you?

Long, lean and quiet, all looking rather like Gary Cooper, they used to come into the coffee bars where we went for breakfast in British Columbia. We slept in motels, and very comfortable they were. It was fun, exploring each new unit of bedroom, bathroom and sitting room to see which had the most gadgets – I still have a pair of paper mules for the bathroom marked Ranch Motel, Clinton, B.C. Perhaps because these in Western Canada were my first motels, I always had a faint sense of magic when we turned the key in our own front door and went in, to find all this imitation domesticity apparently maintained without human hands, as we never saw anybody, to be the temporary home of a long line of anonymous nomads who never met each other.

I don't remember our dinners, perhaps they are best forgotten (until we reached Vancouver and Victoria and ate Chinese) but I remember those breakfasts. We would pack and leave the motel – I felt we were on the run as there was no one to say goodbye to – and drive to the nearest town. Very small towns, just a main street, with the raised sidewalks to keep you clear of the mud in winter, still looking much as they had when horses were tethered all along outside the saloons. Now there are cars nuzzling each other there instead. The coffee house has a long central counter for people to sit on three sides, and lots of shining machines from which you may obtain various kinds of food and drink and indigestion tablets. There are human attendants too, who cook you crisp waffles with the utmost precision. Then you help yourself to the maple syrup from tricky little dispensers set along the counter at short intervals, so that should the place be full, no one need let his waffle cool before filling all its honeycomb cells with the syrup. This is accompanied by black coffee from an urn, and you add the cold milk (called cream as in U.S.) from another dispenser.

The juke-box stands against the wall, and the cowboys who happened to be in town would drift silently over to it when they had ordered their breakfast (their walk as distinctive without their horses as a sailor's without his ship), put in a coin, press the button, and come back to sit at the counter and listen to the dreamy, endless, timeless cowboy rhythms, the songs of loneliness. Once two American commercial travellers came in, and back-slapped each other up to jollity as desperately as two men meeting in a desert, while the quiet Canadians sat around eating and watching them; though this was probably less a national difference than the difference between city and country.

The Indians we met later. Driving North up the old Caribou Trail, we would leave the car sometimes to walk for a while along the original track where it wound through trees, haunted for ever by the men and horses who had toiled along it in goldrush days. We arrived in Williams Lake on the night before the annual cattle sales, and the town was bursting at the seams with men who had brought cattle in from all over the area. There were great corrals and bivouacs outside the town, and the sidewalks and restaurants and bars were seething and spilling over.

We telephoned the family we were on our way to visit, on a ranch between Williams Lake and Bellakula on the coast, and the unchanged English voice welcoming us came unexpectedly over the phone, knowing his whole life had been lived there. Then we squeezed ourselves into a restaurant and ate I forget what, fascinated to watch the shifting crowd. I had not realized how short Indians are, nor did I then know how far less developed the tribes who stayed in North America are than the tribes who pressed on to the South and evolved great civilizations. (The Indian museum outside Victoria or Vancouver Island was to begin my education.) They cannot take drink, and on this night they were all full of it, celebrating the annual visit to town. The Canadian Mounted Police patrolled the streets, two to a car, men and cars unbelievably elegant, gleaming black and silver uniforms and motors, gliding slowly, keeping a look-out for trouble.

Strolling through the town we found our crowded sidewalk blocked by a confrontation as immobile as a tableau. A Mountie outfacing a drunken Indian. The Indian's arms hung to clenched fists and his head was lowered, as he almost visibly debated whether to hit out, or whether to go along. The Mountie stood relaxed but alert, watching to anticipate the first quiver of decision. He was speaking so quietly you could only just

hear him. 'Now, are you coming along with me? You know
you'll have to in the end, so why not just come along now?
Much better, isn't it? Why not come along? Do we take you
or do you come along? It'll be the same in the end, so why
don't you come along? Save a lot of trouble. Well, are you
coming? Come along with me now.' It was very patient, almost
mesmeric, an extraordinary demonstration of control by personality, by confidence, by experience. At last the Indian, with
almost a wriggle of negation, gave way and shambled un-
steadily off beside him – to sleep it off, and be let out when he
was no longer aggressive.

They say whoever crosses the Frazer River must come back.
Many countries haunt you because they are saturated with
generations of human living, but Western Canada stirs you
by the opposite. This is virgin country. No one has left their
mark here. The country itself is the personality. These forests
go on and on till they dwindle to swamp and tundra and then
the Arctic. The twin threads of railway and road run through
the mountains. The railway chiefs are in their office in
Vancouver every day at the time when the train comes out
of the Rockies. To receive the signal that it has come through.
Every day. Just in case. Human ingenuity has spun this thread
through that immense barrier, but no one can be quite certain

when a slide might start, however vigilantly the slopes are watched on either side, for so many miles.

In warm October weather, the last lingering days of a late Indian summer, I remember this country in three colours; the golden forests, the blue sky, and the white snow on the mountains; also the green of the Frazer River. Each morning, staying with our friends at Chilancoh Ranch, we went out and looked at the sky. When the clouds settled on the mountains we must go, it would mean the end of summer, the beginning of winter. Something decisive, irresistible, like the arrival of an invading army. As people grow older they come to fear the winter. It goes on for so long. At last the break, dissolution into slush, a world of water, then suddenly the miracle of the wild flowers. Before we left Chilancoh they lit the furnace in the central stove, and the heat knocked you back. 'You need it when you come from 40-to-60° below,' our host said. Peonies grow well in that garden, almost the only herbaceous flower to survive the winter.

Fall brings the city slickers out killing in fancy dress, bright colours, so they can shoot at anything that moves without killing too many of each other. The classic story of the man who shot his father mistaking him for a moose. The true story of a hunting party bringing a dead donkey to our friend – his child's donkey – to ask him what it was. They'd shot it 'because they thought it was some kind of deer'.

The beavers are back, we saw the dams they had built in the water.

This solid, capacious log house beside the stream, with that character of its own which a strong home in a lonely country always has, was built by our host's father. He and a group of friends, ex-cavalry officers, had come out here after the First World War to buy land, build homes, and ranch this great plateau. The central living-room is dominated by a painting above the hearth of his mother, who arrived with twenty pairs of shoes from Paris, and broke all the heels in the slats outside the door, and just laughed, and came home to England every year to see her dentist, because the first-class fare wasn't much then and there were still bears in the streets of Vancouver. And she had a Chinese staff. Our beautiful hostess said diffidently, 'Everyone thinks the pioneer women were so tough, but I'm not sure it isn't harder now in some ways. There's no excuse to go home to England, and the fare's so high. When cattle prices are good we just plough the money back into

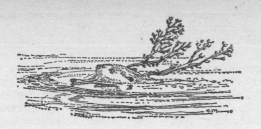

the place, for the boys.' She had met her husband on leave in the Second World War, when he and other sons of the men who had emigrated together came back to England to enlist. They asked, and miraculously succeeded, in keeping together in Tanks as their fathers had been in Cavalry. She had come back with him at the end of the war to spend the rest of her life in this wild and lonely place. Chilancoh had been the end of the world until, just before our visit, the road through to Bellakula had been completed. The telephone had arrived a few years before, and she had planned to celebrate having it by ringing up her brother in Cairo. But while the Exchange was working across the world to connect them, click, click, click, the other new, excited subscribers along the party line took off their receivers to listen-in for company, so that by the time they got Cairo it was too faint to hear her brother.

Their elder son had come to England to agricultural college and in his turn brought a bride back to Chilancoh. They were building a house farther along the valley, and had a baby – the fourth generation. Our host and hostess would have been a spectacular couple anywhere, with their slim lithe height and great good looks, and with complete unselfconsciousness they had remained as English in speech and manner as when they arrived – it would never have occurred to them to think about their behaviour, or to pretend to be what they were not. They had become one of the legends of British Columbia – how no one who had ridden a horse broken by him could feel happy on a horse he had not trained; how he had once wrestled with a grizzly . . . The sons were about half-Canadian; the daughter-in-law was a different kind of English, already the consolidation between her and her mother-in-law was firm and spontaneous – a real thing, a necessary thing. 'Oh, Ma, I'll never be able to cook as well as you do. Someday we'll earn you a Hired-man.' The baby would grow up all-Canadian. The story of Canada in one family.

The morning came when the clouds were on the mountain. We left Chilancoh and drove across Sheep Creek, a very long suspension bridge that had been condemned for many years, but as it was the only way out everyone went on using it, even the loaded cattle trucks, and the trucks that brought supplies to the ranches in the area.

By the time we looked out of the train windows on the journey back from Vancouver to the East, the leaves had vanished, the long snow had begun, the world was black and white and the endless dripping forests stretched to infinity, and bears came out beside the line to see the train go by.

We flew into Mexico City two days before Christmas. Only one's imagination now ghosts behind it the gleaming white Aztec city in the lake. *And when we saw all those cities and villages built in the water . . . it seemed like an enchanted vision . . . that first glimpse of things never heard of, seen or dreamed of before.*

But I remember the modern Mexico City as a panorama which kept me glued to our windows at night. The Hotel Bamer is very strategically placed and we were just the right height up. The city glittered in a huge, perfect semi-circle of lights. Never have I seen a city glitter as brightly as Mexico City in the clear air of 7,434 feet! Those massed lights twinkled so fast one waited for them to leap and dance. Below us in the foreground, framed in the middle of this dazzling mass of diamonds, lies the dark patch of the Alameda Gardens (this is where the great market of Tenochtitlan stood, and later the execution ground of the Spanish Inquisition). The trees appear to be in full leaf, because in this strange climate some trees are shedding their leaves while others are putting forth new ones, and some do both at once. The Gardens only look a mass of darkness by comparison with the sparkle around them, because each tall tree is sprinkled with very tiny lights, a different colour for each tree, so that one is amber, another blue, another red, another white, the lights so small it seems a horde of luminous butterflies have alighted. And in front of the Gardens there glows a hedge of balloons. These are held on long strings by the line of men selling them. The balloons are made in the shapes of men and birds and animals and monsters, and some are life-size. They are multi coloured like a flower market. People buy them to trail out of their car windows as they cruise slowly up and down the Avenue Juarez, packed to overflowing with people who have come into town for Christmas. It is not the fashion here to burst balloons, but to wear them. Some are made into head-dresses which the children wear, so that the face of a strange bird or animal rests above their own – a direct descendant of the feather head-dresses the Aztecs made in very similar designs. Gypsies come into town, and you suddenly fall over one sitting in the slight recess of a shop window, her full skirt swept into a circle round her, and the fact that she is sitting on the dirty pavement with the crowd milling above her, does not prevent her from having a poised, almost flaunting air – an air of enjoying herself. A small child stands beside her, holding a baby in her arms.

On Christmas Eve English friends invited us to their Christmas dinner party. 'But wait a minute before you accept,' they said. 'You may not want to come at all, you may think it's something to avoid at all costs! Just say so, you're coming to stay with us when it's all over, anyhow. But on Christmas Eve we entertain all the family. Do you understand what that means? We have lived in Mexico for three generations, you would not believe how many of us there are. This party ranges from very old people to those for whom it is their first formal dinner. One cousin will have two wives – the one he has divorced and the present one. We shall place them at opposite ends of the room. If you are brave enough to come, you will be the only non-family present. Now you know the worst!'

Of course we went! But first, on that full Christmas Eve, in English spring weather, a light suit, we drove out of Mexico City through a dust-choked slum which indeed appeared to be disintegrating into grey powder, so uniformly colourless and hazed with dust were the close rows of huts. All this was part of the land from which Texcoco Lake had been drained, and whenever there is any wind the dust moves. We visited the monstrous Basilica of Guadalupe on the hill called Tepeyac, and over the vast bare space between gate and church there appeared to be an army of cripples advancing; but no, they were pilgrims covering the 400 yards on their knees. At Teotihuaccân we walked round the Temple of Quetzalcoatl (no wonder the poet Turner made a poem out of Mexican names!). We lunched in a cave restaurant and ate a dish which is served only on Christmas Eve. Called *revuetico*, it is rissoles of dried shrimps pounded and mixed with egg, served in a hot sauce and garnished with what I can only describe as dried grass.

In the afternoon we climbed the Pyramid of the Sun. The statistics stun you: bigger at the base than Egypt's Great Pyramid but not so high; the ceremonial area is two miles by three; two hundred and fifty thousand people lived here. A tunnel reveals the new layer added every fifty-two year

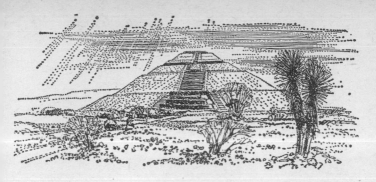

cycle. We walked the broad Highway of the Dead, climbed the Pyramid of the Moon, and from each great stone mountain we surveyed the other, rising unnaturally out of the bare plain. I have never seen fear and blind power – violence – expressed in stone as they are in Mexico. The heads are designed to terrify. The pyramids, these and many smaller ones, are built to be the stage for human sacrifice. Climbing the endless sweep of steps, planned to be crowded with priests and victims, walking through tunnels, out-staring the nightmare faces, one wonders what frenzy drove them to create *like this*?

The Christmas Eve dinner was pure Forsyte. The guests were elegant, very diverse, so numerous that some who had recently married into the family seemed as much strangers as we were. Had we not been told, we should never have guessed they were all connected, except for a gentle interest in spotting each other, a sort of party game, rather like people at a masked ball penetrating each other's disguises. We sat at many small tables in the hall; the dining room was large but not large enough for this gathering. Dinner was basically the traditional English mid-winter feast of roast turkey and Christmas pudding, correctly and beautifully done and therefore delicious, lightened for the milder climate by salads and fruit. The house was decorated with lights and massed flowers, and of course a Christmas tree.

The next night, Christmas night, we went alone to a place we had heard of in the old part of the town, Los Casuilos, which had been started as a soup kitchen during the Revolution, and was now run as a restaurant by a grand-niece of the woman who had run it in revolutionary days. We found it empty except for a young French couple, we thought on

honeymoon. The décor was tiling, the chairs black and painted in bright colours. On the other side of a glass partition, the girl who ran the restaurant was celebrating Christmas with her boy friend and a bottle of wine; behind her was a row of fantastic great cooking pots on a line of stoves. We ate Caldo son Pollo (chicken broth); Guacamole y tostados (avocado salad and toasted tortillas); fried bananas with sour cream, and Mexican coffee, sweet, served in pot-bellied little earthenware jars with narrow tops.

We walked through narrow dark streets, empty except for the occasional drunk sleeping on the pavement, to the Zócalo. This had been the great Aztec square. The cathedral stands where their temple had stood, and the National Palace, taking up the whole of the eastern side of the Zócalo, is built on the site of Montezuma's palace. The present buildings were lined with small spotlights, giving an effect of candlelight. The Avenue Juarez, leading us home to the Alameda Gardens, seemed fuller than ever, if that were possible. We managed to share a taxi with a young Mexican who was showing his little boy the sights – he had been given red gloves, jersey and scarf all to match, and talked all the time of the Superman kit he had in a box, while he carefully trailed his balloon out of the window.

Christmas lasts a long time in Mexico. We knew when the year changed because our friends invited us to see the New Year in at their house in Cuernavaca. I was surprised when my hostess picked out only my cotton dresses for this, but she was right – dropping the 2,376 feet was dropping into full summer. As both families had for the moment had enough of parties and people, the four of us spent New Year's Eve on our own. A wood fire had been lit for gaiety, but the French windows stood wide open. We drank our champagne and kissed each other a Happy New Year, then went out into the warm garden. The men plunged into the pool, while we walked under strange trees and I tried to learn the names of strange flowers; the blue climber on the house was Petrea, the flame trees Spathodia, the Orchid trees Banhinia, with their camel's foot leaf, the red Arum lilies on the terrace were Anthurium, and Calorin (Erythieina) is the one with long brown pods full of red seeds which are threaded for necklaces; its flowers are eaten – red spiky things. A background of Poinsettias grew against a wall.

But it was still Christmas in the small towns and villages as we drove to Veracruz, and then followed the route Cortés had taken back to Mexico City. Indeed, I remember sitting in some bare lounge and thinking that without the coloured paper garlands and artificial flowers, horrid as they were, these empty, old-fashioned hotels would have been pretty depressing; decorations stay up till the end of January, in the streets as well as indoors.

Our friends of Mexico City and Cuernavaca had introduced us carefully to all the main Mexican dishes, cooked correctly by their Indian cook (and the other Indian girl who waited at table giggled deliciously when my husband insisted on try-ing even the hottest things and burned his mouth). There was always a bottle of Tequila on the coffee tray – a lovely coffee tray with tall coffee pot, cream jug and sugar basin of exquisite, very old Mexican silver with gold in the metal which gave it a glow – and a little of it in black coffee seems to me the only good way to drink it (probably therapeutic too).

Even after this favoured introduction to the Mexican cuisine, I found it more a matter of novelty and curiosity than of discoveries I want to go back to. The tortilla is ubiquitous – a pancake of maize flour. I think it is at its best used almost as wrapping paper by the endless street stalls where they take one from the pile and throw it on the smoking stove, flip it over, ladle a filling of meat or chicken with vegetables from another pot on to it, fold it, and put it into the customer's hand; he pays and walks away eating it. An excellent, clean, appetizing way of serving food-in-the-hand. But at sit-down meals the endless pancake makes every dish heavier than it need be. Tameles, tacos, enchillades, tostados, so many intriguing names end up as stuffed pancake. The hot dark brown sauce, Mole, that looks like chocolate, thick and heavy, makes everything it is served with indistinguishable. 'Mole de guajolote' is turkey with mole. Would the turkey without the sauce have either taste or texture? Perhaps not. Perhaps that's why. Frijoles, the small Mexican beans, are another regular, again something thick and floury. I love spiced food, and I love Eastern food, Indian, Chinese and Indonesian. But there seemed to me a unique heaviness about the Mexican table. The beer is good but not the wine, and the wine from Chile, which is very good, seems absurdly expensive. Mexico discourages frivolous imports.

We had been warned, as everyone is, to eat and drink lightly until accustomed to the altitude (digestion taking much longer because of reduced oxygen), especially at night. Looking back with regret, I think I rather overdid this caution. One day after a delicious lunch at a club overlooking the Alameda Gardens – a fish cooked with peppers – I passed course after beautiful course at an Embassy dinner party. I'm sure I could have been more enterprising.

But monotony and stodge set in as we lifted the menus with decreasing hope in the smaller towns of our pilgrimage. The real delight was the fresh limes, served with everything and improving everything, especially soup, and they are the essential heart of the daiquiris which were always our apéritif.

There was glory too. The volcanoes of Popocatapetl and Iztaccihuatl hang over this country. The sky-piercing peak of Popocatapetl, 'the hill that smokes', and beside him the billowing lines of Iztaccihuatl, 'the white woman' – probably because of her mantle of snow. An Indian legend had it that she was the wife of her formidable neighbour. Of course they became people, gods. Their group towers inescapably, you are always aware of them, you can navigate by them. Infinitely various are the lines they make, seen from endlessly changing directions, breathtaking at dawn and sunset, always new. Alive. They seem to spring from the plain without warning, and when Cortés made the extraordinary decision to take his army between them, by the pass which now bears his name, instead of going round, it must have seemed that he was telling them to raid the sky.

From the coast at Veracruz, through Zempoala and Jalapa,

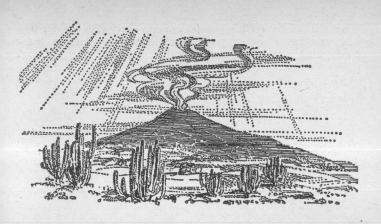

we reconstructed his journey, step by step right up to that pass. At one point we stood in the thin gold grasses of a flat plain, knowing he had made camp there, halting his little army for a whole fortnight. Why? – always in danger and with time pressing. 'Now I understand,' my husband said. 'The country tells me. He *had* to know.' To send out scouts and wait for their return, to tell him where there was water, where the possible routes, where the tribes were, and cover for ambush. Except for two villages which seem to have disappeared, it was possible to follow his entire route. Strangely, some of the tribes have kept their ancient character. In Tlaxcala, it seemed very reasonable that the decision of the Tlaxcalans to support Cortés had been almost the hinge of his fortunes. They are broader-faced, smiling, quicker, more relaxed and confident than the Indians in the Aztec part of the country. They had always stood out against the Aztec empire. Their vigorous, independent city, with a long wall in the governor's palace covered with murals – modern, very strong, as mesmeric as picture-writing, depicting their ancient shrines with their gods streaming across the sky – lies in a dip below scoured chalk hills which mark it for many miles. You drive over the flat country between fields of maize and sugar, golden now, passing the thatched hovels, the men with machetes for cutting the corn, the hobbled donkeys, the loaded trucks, the women always bent forward from the hips by habit of the burden on their backs – baby, shopping, sticks, or just the bags to carry them in – so you feel they could never straighten again, nor ever shed the drab clothes that seem to have grown to them.

(Once, and only once, I had a glimpse of the legendary Indian girl. At Zempoala where, beyond another dusty shack village, we found a whole ceremonial complex of sacrificial pyramids still standing, with a football pitch laid out between them. I climbed the flight of wide steps up to the platform at the top, and hearing laughter and voices, I looked down and through the trees fringing the river I could just see a group of women washing clothes, and patterned by the leaves, the nearest girl's bare head and bare brown shoulders with the sleek black hair flowing over them.)

Approaching Puebla, La Malinche hangs over you, the volcano named for the Indian woman who became Cortés's 'tongue', perhaps the strangest of all women in the sidelines of history, travelling with the Spaniards, interpreting for them, advising them, their contact with all the tribes. Looking back, you can see Orizaba, the highest peak in Mexico; all four volcanoes visible together, topped with snow.

A man ploughing in his own field saw a volcano begin to open in front of his plough, and a friend of ours who saw it six months later said it had grown to a thousand feet. From some angles, in some lights, the jagged edge of the crater at the top of Popocatapetl is very visible. In Mexico City small tremors are a way of life, but a friend who lives there heard (on the radio when in London) that a statue near her home had been toppled from its base – a very big statue. Is this inescapable ever-present menace the explanation of the look on the stone faces, of all the sacrificial pyramids rising from the plain like man-made volcanoes, of the churches where the crucifixes and the statues of martyrs have more blood on them than in any other country? Agonized figures arranged with great realism and detail, elaborately dressed with ribbons in their hair, until in very poor and lonely churches in country places – at La Antigua, for instance, on the coast near Veracruz (which lies in flat sandy country with palm-thatched houses and a curious breed of flop-eared cattle; with fishing boats where the river meanders into the sea, off which lies the rock where Cortés sheltered his ships), the church stands in an empty white square with everything crumbling, by a blue-painted bandstand in a weedy garden; some way from the village's scattered settlements – and has an extraordinary atmosphere. It seems a riot of tortured dolls flung about by frightened children; crude and primitive the figures may be, but they are speakingly powerful, dressed in the bright-coloured scraps from somebody's best dresses. They express injury and despair, they are a desperate cry for help . . . but to whom? Very thin, and very confused, is the layer Catholicism has spread in four hundred years over what went before.

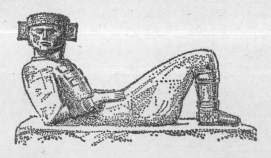

But Puebla, big sophisticated Puebla, was still having Christmas. A charming hotel outside the town, our window framing Popocatapetl over the swimming pool. The barman, very correct in white coat, operated in a small passage-like room off the basement, I never understood why; he mixed superb daiquiris, and you stepped over large white bundles of laundry to reach him. After dinner – a very good chicken tacos – we drove down into the town, to the Zócalo, the central square, where the water of the fountains was lit and the trees festooned with lights. We sat down at a café on the pavement under the arches, in front of a line of shops, to admire the square, and a thin old black-swathed beggar woman drifted by. I gave her a little coin and she seized my hand and kissed it with terrifying passion, then the waiter came and swept her away like a leaf.

After our coffee we walked round the square to the cathedral on the opposite side. Its huge bulk crouched above the square, set very high, black behind all the lights. We climbed the long flight of steps into darkness and quiet above the stream of traffic circling the square, and suddenly caught a strange whiff of hay, and heard munching, and soft movements and rustling. Here were animals, real animals, having their supper and settling themselves for the night. Close beside the cathedral wall, within its precincts, a row of byres had been built for

Christmas, open to the stars, inviolate. In one there was a donkey, in one two cows; then a few sheep, a mule, and a group of young heifers clustered round a new bale of hay. Each moving about in its pleasant, roomy place. This world within a world, the surprise of this Christmas thought; for this I shall always remember Puebla Cathedral with gratitude.

Inside, one remembers only that it is enormous, towering, and there is so much gilding, so much. All that gold taken from the Indians and melted down. Then mined by the conquered Indians. All that gold.

Outside, the animals had stretched themselves out to sleep in their hay-scented rooms, quiet, dark and remote, as we went down again into the river of lights and movement.

We drove up over burnt brown country with birds that looked like buzzards soaring over low hills of bare rock, all brown, brown. Cortés had crumpled a piece of parchment in his hand and flung it down and said, 'That is the map of Mexico.' By hairpin bend after hairpin bend we climbed on to a tilted landscape, up into the clouds, and through a rent in them we looked out of this moist cold loneliness which seemed to imprison us on to a track without end, and over the sheer edge of the road, we saw a bright green sunny valley 3,000 feet below.

We dropped from the plateau where the clouds raced up to the hidden snow peaks, down to crops again, even grass, then to flowers and palms. Through Fortin de las Flores, smothered in roses and carnations. But I remember most vividly one village out of so many – the usual square with its dusty garden, the wide steps up to the white church with ambitious façade crumbling, and a street of shops going up a hill, with many people standing about or sitting on the pavement; an air of sullen inertia. It was one of the few places where I felt uneasy – I think because no one seemed to have anything to do (was it a holiday?) and I wondered what we were doing, invading their lives. Walking past so many eyes; what were they thinking? We stopped and bought some oranges, and talked to the children of a woman sitting on the ground by the fly-blown fruit, and I was glad when she smiled; anything to establish a thread of contact.

Headed for Veracruz where Cortés had landed, we passed from tropical vegetation round Cordoba, crossed with barrancas, with breadfruit and fields of sugar, to wider, more open country, where paeons in broad-brimmed white panama hats herded cattle on Palomino ponies, which they hitched to a tree when they stopped to buy groceries at a roadside store. At last a concrete bridge over a wide river, and a glimpse ahead of white waves breaking. The place of Cortés's first battle, and the tree-ed promontory where he had made his first camp. We saw a boat riding inside the banks, so far inshore it looked aground . . . is this where he anchored his fleet?

The night we returned to Mexico City, I went to the window and saw nothing. After a moment of bewilderment I realized that heavy cloud had obscured all the lights. Then it snowed. The first snow in thirty years. Our friends came to dinner with us our last evening, and later rang up to say they'd got home safely, but there was no electricity because the lines were down, that her husband was sitting in six eiderdowns very cross because the central heating was off; but that the garden looked lovely and she'd woken her maids to look at it because they'd never seen snow before. And now she couldn't get them back to bed because they wouldn't tear themselves away from the window while the flakes were still falling.

Pisco Sour and Conchitas are my culinary discoveries in Peru. Otherwise, it tends to be 'International' menus – 'International', that poor, synthetic, test-tube-bred kind of food, that has spread over the world like algae, and is about as tasteless. (The best South-American dishes I've eaten were in the Costa del Sol Restaurant below the Time-Life Building in New York. Sometimes the more exotic local dishes are only found far from their alleged home, or are they just invented far from home? – what *might* have been done with local ingredients?')

Of course, the good restaurants in Lima serve excellent meals, and I've enjoyed every mouthful of many, but one might have been anywhere – except for the dazzling view of the city at night from the Roof Restaurant of the Crillon Hotel, with the cold little breeze of the air-conditioning always curling round one's neck from the huge plate-glass windows. And I remember breakfast in the garden at Arequipa, when for magic moments the three great peaks, El Misti, Chachani and Pichu-Pichu in turn swam clear of cloud, hanging above one in the sky, unbelievably remote, then drew their vapours round them again.

But Conchitas. Ah! Conchitas . . . They are a small relation of the scallop. They are *not* just small scallops. They are a separate branch of the family, not only small, but very tender and sweet. Six as an hors d'oeuvre before dinner, or for a light lunch on a breathless Lima day, when the permanent stationary umbrella of cloud presses down on the city. Usually they are grilled, which I like best, though they can be served in various sauces, and one spirited friend preferred them raw, like oysters. I never tired of them. I left them with regret. I should like some now.

Pisco Sour we drank first at the house of a friend, who said, 'It's a waste of time mixing Pisco Sours singly, I always mix doubles now.' Pisco is the national brandy. Pisco Sour is made by adding fresh lemon juice and white of egg, whisked in an electric mixer, with a few drops of angostura sprinkled on top, where they lie like little pink dimples in the white foam. Surprisingly rough, remote bars have the ingredients and equipment always ready. The glory of Pisco Sour (apart from its fresh and delicious taste) is that it lifts your body and spirit from exhaustion or horror, and yet leaves no after effects (in proportion to other spirits; I did not pursue this beyond reason).

Every journey ended with Pisco Sour. When we achieved Cajamarca at last, just before nightfall, just before our petrol ran out, and Ralph relaxed at the wheel for the first time in many hours, I prised myself up from the hand-grip, on which I had been chiefly riding, and climbed stiffly up the steps to a large, impressive, but rather municipal-looking building in the hope that it was an hotel. A big lounge – hotel or club? – very dark, quite empty. A Spanish boy reading a paper behind a counter slipped to his feet and greeted me with obvious surprise. Yes, it was an hotel. He pushed the familiar registration form towards me. As I filled it in a middle-aged man, thick-set, white-haired – German? – emerged from the manager's office, switched on a lot of lights and stood peering over my shoulder as I wrote. 'Ah!' he said. 'An English lady! That explains everything.'

He asked me how I'd got there, and I explained I had a husband outside in a car, perhaps someone could go for the luggage? Yes, yes, he would send someone, but how had we got there? The road was cut by the worst floods in thirty years, no trucks had got through to them. All this northern mountain area of which Cajamarca at 9,000 feet is the centre, is supplied by trucks, trucks as personal as ships, each with her name painted on the front. El Rehelde. Un Amigo Mas. El Optimista. Chicho. El Trovador. Carlos Enrique. El Batman. El Errante. Virgin de L'Accension. Youba. El Buen Amigo. Mercedes del

Sol. El Prominente. Moralitos. Faustito. Purisma Concepcion. El Angel. El Conductor. Colosa del Rodos. Wilfredo. Elsinore de la Solidas. El Yaoo. Le Pederosa. Doris. No railway, no airfield is possible among these mountains.

And yet, the manager persisted, the trucks that had left that morning on the downward journey had not come back – had we met them? With some pride I told him we had indeed met the downgoing trucks (long, long ago it seemed, quite early in the day, in sunshine and great heat, when we light-heartedly thought we were through the worst) and they had stopped to ask us – us! – how to get through, and we had been able to tell them, and they had recognized the names we gave them, and unhesitatingly taken our route.

We'd been lucky. Setting out gaily from Chiclayo for this great ascent into the cloud, we suddenly found the coastal road, the Pan-Americano, cut right across by a roaring torrent. Also inspecting this astonishing sight, presumably to see if it threatened her property, was a very elegant woman in riding clothes, who said, 'Do you *really* want to get to Cajamarca? Because, if so, there is a way. Go back a little, leave the main road and turn up the side of the hills to the village of Chepen. From there climb again and go through the Hacienda Talamba. There is a farm path along the top, and when you see you're past this break in the road, you can find your way down through the fields until you see a bridge to bring you back to the road.'

All this we did – a very narrow ridgy track, between scrub trees and huts and pigs (for miles and miles it was the embankment of a long-dead Inca canal), then back over a somewhat flimsy bridge – and went on our way gaily, even stopping to eat some oranges, and to photograph two people working in a paddy field. Then realized we had shifted on to a much smaller-scale map, and were barely started on the ascent to Cajamarca. Continuing rather seriously, we were stopped by some railway men at a crossing and told the road was cut again by the floods. But they too were helpful. 'The train will be through in a few minutes. It's the only train – then you may go along the railway track till you are past the break in the road!'

We bumped over the sleepers of the single track, through a tunnel, over the girder bridge, the flooded river below us, then found our road again. The last village, Chilete, was beginning to crumble into the water. (Later we saw in the papers that it was a disaster area.) Then we really started climbing.

I remember a sudden cloud of small green parrots exploding across the road and vanishing over the gorge. I remember looking up and seeing a blur of fresh green among the peaks way up in the sky ahead. I thought it was a trick of the light. But no, it was one of the Alpine meadows. Endlessly we wound and climbed. It grew colder. Patches of mist blotted us out. On one side the edge of the road had frequently subsided down the gorge. On the other, slides had brought the hillside down on to the road in a pile of stones. Then we came to a place where the slide from above was opposite a subsidence of the outer verge, so there was no road. Fortunately it was possible to turn off on to a track which had presumably been the old footpath before the road was built. We steered between stones and boulders in thick greyness, wondering how much of this was mist, how much approaching night, and how much the mud on our headlights, which now seemed about one candlepower. Also wondering how much petrol we had. We would not, could not, stop, mesmerically intent to see if we could indeed get to Cajamarca – which now seemed an ever-receding place of myth and legend – or if some final hazard would strand us in this desolate loneliness for the night.

Then at last we saw her, across a great valley, lying against the hills. Cajamarca, towards which Pizarro had poured his troops down the Pass – that Pass there – with flamboyant stage-craft, watched by Atahualpa nursing his septic wound at the hot springs on the other side of the city. The city of the massacre, the room filled with gold, the final sickening and destruction and despair.

'You must not be afraid because of the cracks in the wall

77

Washed-out road to Cajamarca, Peru

of your bedroom,' the manager said. 'It is only the last earth-quake, we have not had time to repair them yet. All is safe now.'

Then the bare green Bar, with three local men playing dominoes, and the Spanish boy who had first welcomed me smiling behind the counter and whizzing up lovely, lovely Pisco Sours.

I'm told it was not really spring. Weather in Peru is patchy; when it's summer in the plains it's winter in the Sierra. But what else could it be, this vernal ritual we found happening all around us in the high country round Cajamarca? The coming of the rains, re-starting the annual cycle of life and growth? What is that but spring?

The month was February, the altitude 9,000 feet. The alpine meadows stood rich with clover hay – like English fields, but their hedges were cactus – and little groups of Indian women strolled through them, chatting and weaving, guarding their straggling mixed flocks. Once I counted eight different kinds of animals the women were driving – if anything so leisurely could be called driving. Llamas predominated, but there were also alpacas, goats, sheep, donkeys, a pony, a dog or two and some ducks. The group of women chattered in Quechuan like magpies, and as they walked always their fingers flew in the white wool they were weaving on to a stick. Short and squat in their bunchy bright-coloured clothes, hatted under a scarf, bright eyes darting, always the busy fingers which seemed to have a life of their own moved in the little white clouds of wool.

We first realized something special was happening when we set out to visit an old Indian burial place about 9 kilometres north-east of Cajamarca. We had seen pictures of this Necropolis, a rocky hillock with windowed burial places, near the Hacienda Otuzco.

Driving towards it, we found the track alive with little groups of Indians, men and women, who were going there too. The women had such pretty faces between the jaunty hats and the squat bodies in voluminous clothes; bare-footed, with gold ear-rings, sometimes very heavy. Some of the men were already a little drunk – some more than a little, tottering and weaving, and the women supporting them. A few men were on horseback, riding without stirrups, or with a heavy tri-angular toe-grip. Very fine they looked with their wide hats and short brown poncho-like jackets. One group had a banjo, and some a pipe and drum, and they walked dancingly to the music. Many groups carried green branches, large ones to simulate a whole tree. They were of eucalyptus (strange foreigner in this land!). In a field beside the road we saw a group who had set up their tree and were dancing round it. The whole countryside seemed alive with little groups bearing a green bough, unhurried but purposeful, all making their way to the sepulchre hill.

When we reached it, we climbed a short distance up the narrow winding path between bushes. The sepulchres are on the south-east side of the hill, and are very strange, as though lines of jagged holes had been torn out of the naked rock.

Through trees, and half-hidden by the curve of the hill, we saw there was a crowd at the top, and heard their music, the high queer sound of the bamboo pipe, and the drum.

We did not go up. Some mutual instinct, less of nervousness than of respect, made us turn back down the path before the next group entered it. I think we would have been quite all right, the ones we'd passed on the road hadn't seemed to mind us – even the mounted ones, even the drunks. We had no part in this, we were extraneous, perhaps invisible. But they have so little, why should we pry at this, without understanding? All over the high mountain country of the sierra, groups were setting up their trees, with music and dancing, but those who were near enough came to this once sacred place. Still? Again? . . . Why?

We circled the tracks round the hillock and through the village of Otuzco, watching the processions converge. These people seemed happy, as though they knew somewhere to escape from the present, and were going there.

As we drove back to Cajamarca we saw the men who had dropped out lying beside the road quietly sleeping, or just sitting dreamily in the long grasses. The drink is Chica (pronounced Chicha), a corn spirit brewed much the same as in Inca times. We had seen it being ladled out of a big bowl as we drove through the poorer part of the town. It seemed to leave a happy, gentle drunkenness, we saw no instance of belligerence, nor any tautening or sparking that might lead to it, nor even a raised voice or a rough gesture. The people were relaxed and friendly, we felt no unease at being the only strangers. So different from the quick latent fierceness one is always conscious of among the Indians in Mexico. All through their history the Indians of Peru have been gentler tribes, usually to their undoing. (A Peruvian anthropologist in Lima said to my husband, 'We don't have bad epidemics in Peru – even the germs get tired!')

As we entered the town down the long approach road of small shops and houses, I glimpsed through a half-open barn door a man and a woman dancing. Facing each other a couple of feet apart, they trod with absolute concentration a formal, stately measure, and all round the bar a thick ring of people watched them, silent too.

Again we could not – could not – go back and peer in at this ancient, timeless thing. The air tingled with the sense of festival.

I asked the manager of the hotel about the processions. 'It is nothing, madame,' he said contemptuously. 'They want an excuse to get drunk, that is all.'

The next morning, which was Sunday, I woke to music. I had been conscious of a church bell ringing, but the music growing towards us was a high thin pipe and the drum. One of our bedroom windows looked down over a side street leading to the main square; that square which is a quadrangle now, but which had been a triangle when Pizarro trapped Atahualpa there. Below our window passed a ragged procession of four. Two men carried between them, on poles resting on their shoulders, a small open ark with a figure of the Virgin inside. It swayed with the movement of their walking. On their right marched a man holding on his right wrist – or possibly strapped to it – a small drum which he played with the fingers of that hand, while he blew on a pipe which he held in his left hand. Behind them, but dominating them, walked the fourth man, and he played an immensely long pipe. Eight feet of bamboo it was, with a trumpet-shaped piece at the end. We followed their progress through our window on the other side of the room, looking over the square. They entered the

83

church of St Francis as the clock struck 7.30, and as they entered the church bell stopped ringing.

I have since learned from a professor of comparative religions that the procession of pipe and drum is one of the most ancient Indian ceremonies, and that 'one of the oldest engravings we possess shows the tall Inca striding ahead of his people blowing the long trumpet, followed by his fat little wife beating the drum!' He added enviously that we were lucky to have seen what we had.

Back in Lima, they tell you the Indians are mainly outside the economy of the country, that the Mestizo (mixed Indian and Spanish blood) is the hope of the future. The pure Quechuan, surviving chiefly round Puno and the country near Lake Titicaca, can die of malnutrition sitting beside the great herds they do not own, and from which they seldom think of stealing. Sitting on the ground in that high country which has such an extraordinary sense of open-ness, as though it were near the sky. As though time had not arrived.

Yet on the reed islands in Lake Titicaca, the Uru Indians, who seldom visit the mainland, consider the Indians who live there to be degenerate!

Even in the market at Puno, the Quechuans have their atmosphere of smiling, unhurried pleasantness. The women, in this area always wearing their tremendously becoming little bowler hats tied on with a scarf (which you see them wearing indoors – and it is rumoured even in bed), sit on the ground with their goods beside them. I bought a poncho of soft llama wool in a fascinating design of white and brown which I wear often, and like better than the sophisticated ones made to instructions for sale in the shops and hotels. The colours the Quechua wear are very rich and satisfying, particularly the many shades of red. I remember in the market a woman sitting with her little girl lying face-down across her knee, occupying the time usefully between customers by picking ticks out of the child's head. Before her were spread her wares for sale – a long tray of different little pans of dye in powder form. I counted *seven* different reds!

The tribes united under the Incas are all mixed now, but occasionally you see a startlingly perfect physical type. We drove out from Cusco in drizzling rain to see a famous Inca fountain. The road had been an Inca road, and the fountain is built flat into the side of the hill from which the water comes. Tourists from Cusco come here, and the muddy earth in front of the fountain was trampled and littered with banana skins and Kodak cartons. Standing in the middle of it were two little Indian boys, begging. Behind them was the exquisite workmanship of their ancestors, and they had the glowing dark golden skin I only saw once again, in some crowd in a city in another part of the country. I don't know what tribe had this special and wonderful skin colour, which appears occasionally after centuries of breeding with other tribes, but it is startling and beautiful. They stood in rags among the litter, and they were golden. Civilization comes to the children of the Sun!

Some of the Quechua come down to the cities, and live in flimsy bamboo shelters on the outskirts, which because of over-crowding and lack of facilities become slums, and many die early of respiratory diseases. The average lung capacity of the Indian up in the Sierras is almost a third larger than normal. But when they come down to the plain it gradually reverts to normal, so it appears to be a functional adaptation of the individual, not a difference in the racial physique. The great slum on the slope near Lima will become very valuable in time, they say, because of its proximity to the capital, and the Indians will be able to sell their patches of ground for quite a lot.

'But many of them don't seem to care about making money and bettering themselves.'

They just want to be left alone.

Some names always fall heavily, laden with events that have happened there. Sailing into Cherbourg on a Sunday morning when all the church bells are ringing, bending over the chart and seeing the names St Lo and Carenton . . . this was the American Airborne landing ground in 1944. Driving through Holland – can Eindhoven, Niemagen, Arnhem ever become ordinary words again? – or S'Hertogenbosch, the junction town that wrecked everything because it was not taken first, and the dyke roads lying so high, just sitting targets? and the dumps of rusted metal in the fields which were the aircraft I'd seen setting out from Wiltshire in the sunshine. Won't the name 'Bastogne' always strike like a gong?

'This is the only war there's any point in being a paratrooper!' they'd said when they arrived in Wiltshire in the autumn of '43. 'Next time there'll be something else, parachute jumping will be commonplace, a cold potato. But now – it's interesting.'

Their only boast was that they were all volunteers, they came from every corner of the United States.

Suddenly our villages and fields and lanes were full of greygreen uniforms with big pockets, and the beautiful soft leather boots, essential for safe jumping, as cherished and personal as the longbows before Agincourt. Docile as friendly panthers, each found an English home in which he was welcomed. No foreign unit can ever have been absorbed into a whole countryside so quickly.

They gave enormous parties in the great house which was

now their Headquarters. We (young wives waiting out the war in a village, their husbands overseas, some prisoners; the ladies of the big houses who had twenty officers billeted on their top floor and a camp of men in the grounds; village girls; girls picked up in the nearest town) – we were conditioned by four years of war, loneliness, anxiety, small rations, no luxuries. We went blinking and unprepared into the great hall blazing with uncountable candles, a fire of whole branches pushed gradually into the hearth as big as a room. Against the panelled walls hung the armour of Cromwell's soldiers who had once been billeted here. Overhead floated the vast open parachutes in many colours, used for dropping supplies. We danced and drank Bourbon, 'but there's Scotch if you prefer it, or gin, anything you like.' Long white cartons full of cigarette packets were left casually beside us – Lucky Strike, Camels, Old Gold, Chesterfield (we were used to queueing for ten). There was great courtesy, almost an apology, in their giving. The booklet they'd been issued with before leaving the States, telling them how to treat us when they got over here, was rather good. 'Do not make the mistake of thinking these people are cissy-pants because they are quietly spoken. Remember they have taken their voice and their ways to the uttermost parts of the earth.'

The spread on the table was unbelievable – was there so much food, so many things to choose from, in the world? We weren't undernourished – we'd just forgotten about Plenty. The huge white cloth covered with unfamiliar dishes, all colourful and decorated. I don't remember eating much, I just remember how it looked.

So all through that winter the C47s circled overhead, and some mornings the queue of men in the canteen had a curious, depleted look, and one knew there had been a night jump (we should have guessed D-Day for them would be at night).

But other nights we danced under the parachutes in a white dazzle of candlelight, and sometimes exploring the legendary house, came upon some little room where a few of the para-troops, drunk, were singing their terrible song:

> 'Blood on the parachute and
> Blood on the grass . . .'

The tempo of the parties increased as the tension rose towards the unknown, inevitable Jump, wondered about, talked about occasionally, toasted; the purpose of being here; the Jump into occupied Europe.

The Christmas night party was radiant. The unspoken thought – for whom is this the last Christmas, and all so far from home? – gave it the warmth and glow of a fairytale.

But the last party in the spring was held on an invisible tightrope; obviously it couldn't be far off now. This party had to be the most of everything, the last word, the ultimate. The tension twanged. They somehow got enough fuel to heat the indoor swimming-pool, and the steam rose in the dim hot light like a ghostly miasma. In the chapel someone was playing the organ quietly in the dark for his own amusement, and little groups wandering through the house paused to listen for a few minutes then wandered on. In the ballroom a man down on one knee, supporting on the other the head and shoulders of a girl, was pouring a glass of wine very carefully over her face, like an oblation.

The next morning in the village I met a friend who had also been at the party – at all their parties. She said: 'I've already heard so many things about last night from people who weren't there – I'm beginning to wonder if I was there!'

Then they vanished. The camps stood empty except for a skeleton staff. Then on the 6th of June we heard on the 8 a.m. BBC News: 'In the early hours of this morning, units of Allied Airborne Forces were parachuted behind the enemy lines in Normandy.'

Their HQ was still with us. They were in radio contact. News of individuals leaked through, and were passed on to their particular friends, their 'family'. Every few days we knew the casualty lists.

Then their replacements arrived. *Replacements?* These new men began to tell us about life in America and about parachute jumping. We tried to listen politely out of kindness, but we knew it all by heart.

Then their wounded began to dribble back – those red corduroy hospital dressing gowns! the crutches propped against the cottage doors, the eye-patches. At last we heard they had been relieved, a ground unit had got through to them, they were coming home. Home? We sounded the few who were here already as to whether they'd be offended to find a Welcome Home! sign up, as we were not their real home. But no, they thought they'd like that a lot. So a big banner saying

Welcome Home was slung across the village street between the medieval gables.

They came gently, in a kind of bewilderment. 'Is that banner put up there for *us*?' they asked incredulously. Eisenhower had decorated them, Max Taylor had brass bands to meet them at the coast, but they hadn't expected us to notice. Their eyes came back slowly to normal things. The home-coming party was quite different. A kind of astonishment, a benison was upon us all. So much had happened for which, after their long preparation, they were unprepared. Chiefly the civilian snipers; finding the body of a much-loved priest hanging by his heels from a tree beside the road with his throat cut (their chaplains of all denominations jumped with them and jumped unarmed). The behaviour of the French: 'They shut themselves up in their houses and wouldn't even give us a glass of water for a wounded man, or tell us the way.' But a young company commander who, at the end of a day's fighting to take a little town, had collected his dead and laid them all together in a corner of the square, and covered them with a tarpaulin he got from a garage, found in the morning the tarpaulin completely covered with flowers, put there by the townspeople during the night. Everything was contradictory, confused.

Then the discoveries about each other, in the long period of holding with their inadequate arms the objectives they had taken – the thing they had been told throughout their training they would never be asked to do. 'It's funny about him, when the fighting was on no one saw him, his men thought he was dead. Then he bobbed up afterwards – must have passed the time in a shell hole!' 'That hoodlum's the one who kept us going more than anyone. I tell you! – he always turned up with the right silly joke just when you felt you couldn't go on.' 'You know that one who shot the cat and all her kittens behind the barn, said it was for practice? – Well, he was just like that with prisoners. We had to hold him, I think he went mad. He's got a decoration, but I don't believe his story. We never saw him when we needed him.' The long search for a greatly loved battalion commander whose body was never found, though some of his men went back later and searched every inch of the ground; only his jump-jacket, shot right across, was found in a tree. He was listed Missing, believed killed; and later, Killed. The long rangy C.O. of the regiment who swum a river to find out what was happening on the other side.

90

For the home-coming party it was full summer, and the doors and windows stood open to the gardens. There was less drinking and nobody sang the song – it was unnecessary now the thing had actually happened. Some of the girls whose friends had been killed were there, not for gaiety but for companionship, to be again free of that company, and they were looked after unobtrusively but very carefully. The familiar faces missing seemed only absent by chance, not far away. Everybody had died a little in the endless Normandy rain. There was one boy who'd hardly spoken since he came back, and one or other of his friends was always beside him – 'He'll be all right, we're just keeping an eye on him till he comes round.'

Ahead lay the next jump. (A limpid September morning when endless skeins of C47s would stream off over our heads. The jump into the Dutch Salient, when the girls and boys of Eindhoven bicycled out to meet them because 'they looked so beautiful, floating down in the sunshine, we'd waited so long!' A jump like an exhibition, after the Normandy one when they'd gone down into flak like the lights of a town. But the fighting came later, during the long struggle to join up with Arnhem; again the dragged-out time, the wet, the smell, the great black hogs they saw feeding on the bodies of their dead. And ahead again the bitter Christmas holding of Bastogne, when the C47s set off incessantly from our hill in hopeless snow-fog to try and reach them with supplies.)

All this was waiting, but the night of the home-coming party no one looked ahead. It must be the last time; the HQ would now move forward, they would not come back again. The parachutes would not float like giant flowers above Cromwell's armour again, but become just another picture in the long memory of this house, which would itself be remembered, looking like this, by men all over another continent.

The spread of foods on the white tables was familiar to us now, we picked and chose our favourites. New candles were stubbed again and again into the guttering ends, so their massed rows never diminished.

At last we came out sleepily to see the first daylight creeping over the lawns. Getting us all back to our scattered homes had always been a problem. 'We don't use transportation – we jump!' they'd said in grim apology when they first came. I remember once being picked up bodily and dropped gently on to rugs in the back of a 15-cwt truck; going home in an ambulance – that had been winter, lovely and warm! And Jeeps, Jeeps . . .

Home along the empty lanes and heavy green of that moist summer, while the morning light grew clearer over the fields where they'd trained.

> 'Blood on the parachute and
> Blood on the grass and
> Blood on the paratrooper's boot.
> Oh, oh! What a hell of a way to die.'

PART III

THE OPAL-COLOURED LAND

(We eat Australian)

I cannot pretend I approached my father's country without
emotion. I never knew my father, who died when I was six
months old. My mother never went to Australia, and what she
had learned from my father were the boyhood memories of a
man who had left home early, lived his short life in many
other countries and never gone back.

What was it like – this remote fifth continent on which
many desperate and a few eager people had been dumped to
make what they could of it?

On Dunk Island out in the Great Barrier Reef I lay on the
verandah looking through a pattern of branches across a strip
of white sand to the sea and on the other side the blue coast
of Australia. So beautiful. The little crabs, red and black and
transparent white, sped and burrowed and escaped each other
in the sand and the mutton birds called in the trees, and I
looked and looked at the beautiful blue coast, that deadly
dangerous, killer coast. Walking the deep-packed leaves of the
forest paths under the screen of strange trees that protect you
from the tropical sun, watching the unbelievable butterflies of
Dunk Island (huge as birds, scarlet, blue, yellow, black, white
and every pattern) gaps between unfamiliar leaves in the lush
rain forest framed that coast.

The little Cessna had put us down in the grass ride which
is the runway, and two deeply tanned young men in coloured
sarongs put our luggage in a Land-Rover lined with white dust-
sheets. This is the island where E. J. Banfield lived and wrote
Confessions of a Beachcomber. His grave is in a little glade
near the hotel which was once his house, and bears these
lines:

'If a man does not keep pace with his companions perhaps
it is because he hears a different drummer. Let him step to
the music which he hears.'

Our room was a wooden cabin between pine trees and sea.
A bowl of tropical fruit to welcome us and hibiscus flowers
tucked into the coloured towels. All one side, windows look-

93

ing across the sea towards the low blue hills of Queensland.
I thought: 'There is Australia, waiting.' You could even lie in
bed and look at it by moonlight. We walked barefoot to the
dining room, stopping to knock the sand out of our toes before
going in. There had been a spell of bad weather and most of
the tourists had cancelled, leaving us and a handful of others
feeling like private guests of the charming people who ran the
hotel. The weather had cleared as we landed and I cannot
imagine Dunk Island without sunshine.

It was difficult to wake up early enough to see the sun rise,
sleeping to the soft rustle of the little waves and sometimes
waking to watch the moon changing the patterns of trees and
sea and coast (it was early March, late summer). Breakfast was
fun in the dining room of Banfield's old house, a room just
not over-decorated with many-coloured coral and seaweed and
seaflowers and shells and curious bits of driftwood. You helped
yourself to coffee bubbling on the hotplate, cold fruit drinks,
cereals, eggs and bacon, mutton chops, fruit, an English breakfast with bits of lunch thrown in. Lunch one came to dazed
with sun out of the mid-day torpor of the world, longing
for the cold light wine, piling the lovely choice of salads.
There was always one hot dish and cold meats. Dinner was
less good. But it was served by pretty girls in sarongs and
flowers and bare feet, and torches were lit along the edge of
the sea and there was always a pleasant wine to give heart and
gaiety to the meal. Every day 'Barrier Reef fish' figured on the
menu. This was always two pieces fried in batter. Batter is an
obsession in Australia. We became adept at slitting it and slipping it off and rescuing the fish inside as automatically as one
peels shrimps. I could never understand why unfailingly each
night one of my two pieces was good and the other insuffi-
ciently thawed out from the deep freeze. Delicious oysters
were caught from the quay within a stone's throw of the
dining room. You could go and collect your own while you
bathed.

Coming south down the Barrier Reef (I was slow to grasp
that south means cooler and north hotter) we stopped on
Heron Island. This is a coral island and I missed the tropical
glamour of Dunk. I had not realized how coral is visibly alive,
opening all those little mouths to every incoming tide, closing
them to a touch. The Crown of Thorns, the starfish that
threatens the Great Barrier Reef, had not arrived here.

The occupation on Heron Island is swimming and wading

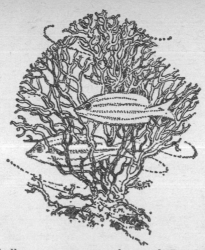

out in the shallow water to see the coral. But I saw the sea slugs, great fat lumps, just alive, half-buried in the sand all around, everywhere, and screamed for a helicopter to take me out because there seemed barely room to pick one's way between them back to the clean dry sand. 'They won't hurt you, they don't sting' didn't comfort me. I prefer to do my coral watching, and see all the bright coloured fish that dart through the coral, from a glass-bottomed boat.

One wonderful thing chanced for us on Heron Island – the annual emergence of the baby green turtles. Suddenly a whirl-pool starts in the dry sand up among the trees and grass at the top of the beach, a swirling circular disturbance growing from a dot to the size of a very large dinner plate. Then the strong, dark, rubbery little creatures begin to emerge, a few inches long, sandwiched between their oval shells which are firm but not yet brittle. Each lifts his head for a first look round, then turns unerringly towards the sea. If, as on this occasion, it is low tide, they have a long, hard journey over the rocks. As their instinct is to go straight to the water they will struggle with a precipice above them very persistently before deflecting to right or left and will explore every possible opening to get back on course. It is irresistible to lift one over its insuperable barrier a few inches high. From this it is a short step to carrying them down to the sea. Soon all the children were filling pockets, caps, buckets with them and launching

each one carefully. Once in their natural element they swim off very strongly – a good adult human swimmer can only just pace them. They lift their tiny flat heads from time to time to look around in a delightfully social way. The seagulls and a few herons swoop overhead, tantalized to fury by the protective presence of the humans. The multitude swarming down over the rocks is an almost terrifying outburst of nature's profligacy, but only a tiny proportion survive to reach maturity. Nest after nest swirls to the surface and the whole beach seems alive with their separate migratory columns. To go back to source and watch a nest erupting is hypnotic. They pour up. It is impossible there should be so many. Still they come.

In spring – September, October – the great green mother turtles come to their chosen islands, climb up the beach and lay their eggs deep in the sand, then return to the sea. For six months everyone walks regardless over the sand. Then the day comes when they boil up to the surface.

Apparently lights deflect and confuse them. Our cabins were just above the beach and people in a neighbouring cabin who'd left a light on found their balcony invaded with tiny determined turtles battering at the glass. So they spent a busy night turning them – extinguishing the light in the room and leading the hordes down to the sea with torches which, they said, they followed, till the mass movement was re-established in the right direction.

We were lifted out of Heron Island in a near gale and a certain atmosphere of anxiety, because just at that time the previous year the Reef had been hit by a cyclone which caused terrible destruction. I did not really expect the helicopter to arrive, but the strange little moth fluttered down on to its circular landing patch on the beach and our luggage was carried out through a film of blown sand. I had never been in a helicopter before and it was an old one. I didn't think anything so fragile could hold its course against the violence of the wind. But it did. Inside that flimsy cage was silence and peace. Beautifully flown, she went straight as an arrow to the mainland over the boiling reef.

There is much to be said for entering a country by its major city. You see the end product, how far they have come at this moment. You can then work outwards to discover the land and people who produced the cities.

Australian cities are the cities of the square-rigged ships. They are the harbours the square-riggers could put in to.

Flying into Sydney is breathtaking by day or by night. The great plane swings for you to see the whole panorama of the city with its water and trees. We saw it first at sunset, dyed with the last glow of the day's light. Another time we flew in at night, when they turn off the interior lights of the aircraft to make more brilliant the pattern of the city's lights. Surely jewelled cities from the sky are one of the few new beauties of our time to set against so much ugliness! Later, sailing in Sydney harbour, I realized how appropriate is the conception of the controversial new opera house. Seen from boat level it looks indeed like a pack of sails in motion, so fitting among all the other sails. The spirit of Sydney Harbour.

Twice we ate at the revolving restaurant – the Summit – once by day and once by night, always torn between the pleasure of our host and hostess's company, the panorama of Sydney below us moving round at exactly the right pace, and the food. Here I ate my first barramundi and read: *Fish n' chips (Served at your table wrapped in the London Times. Traditional.)* promised for 'English week'.

In Brisbane we ate mud crabs, large and delicious in spite of their unattractive name, and were taken out to Lone Pine to visit the Koala Bear reserve.

Of course it is horrible that koalas were shot out for their soft fur, and the right of any species to survive has nothing whatever to do with whether humans 'like' them or not. But if ever there was a creature nature had tired of, surely this is it. The idea of their being 'cuddly teddy bears' is grotesque when you see the size of the scimitar claws on their

stretchy long-fingered feet, claws that can kill a dog, can even disembowel a kangaroo. But what makes them repulsive is their lifeless passivity. They are clustered like burrs all over the tree which they are gradually stripping bare. One is stuck to the tree, another on his back, another on that one's back, sometimes four or five deep, great lumps of them. The keeper plucks off the top one and shows it, then sticks it back; even its eyes do not flicker. Presumably they hold on by their claws, or by muscles, but the effect is of suction; they seem things, not creatures.

The head keeper is extremely knowledgeable and interesting. He is trying to re-establish koalas in the wild and in spite of the difficulty of following this up, as of course they scatter and disappear, he has found gum trees eaten in an area where he had loosed koalas, and knows he is to some extent succeeding. Apparently the extreme passivity of these at Lone Pine is not because they are in a reserve, nor because they are nocturnal. They do not seem to pay much attention to day or night, he says, but wake up when they are hungry, eat some leaves, and go to sleep again. When a tree is bare they have to move to the next. Having eaten, they fall asleep with a paw left at the position it was in last, so their tree is spiky with outflung feet of sleeping bears. The final nightmare touch was that it is the tradition of Lone Pine to have an Alsatian, simply because the original superintendent had one. This dog (presumably castrated), though potentially a fine one, seemed as lifeless as the koalas, without a flicker of that alertness which normally characterizes an Alsatian to the day of his death. His only occupation is to get up when told and have a koala clamped on his back and parade with it for the benefit of such tourists as wish to take a photograph of this unnatural sight, which most seem to do. I found it a deeply depressing place.

We flew up to Cairns on the coast of Northern Queensland and arrived at night in a tropical downpour. People who live there are so used to this that they stand out in the deluge holding one's luggage. Raincoats would be insufferable. Better to pour with rain than with perspiration; it will soon dry anyhow. The roads were awash the next morning but mercifully the sky was clear. Ralph had chartered a little plane from Bush Pilots Airways to fly over the coast and reef where Cook had achieved his perilous arrival. We waited anxiously in our thinnest clothes at the little hut which is the office of Bush Pilots. There was the tiny aircraft. Here was the pilot (Qantas pilots like to work a stint with Bush Pilots to rediscover what flying was all about before they became chauffeurs). We hung about while he made endless telephone calls to get weather clearance. At last . . .

I had never been particularly interested in Cook, nor read anything about him. But flying North from Cairns to Cooktown over the Barrier Reef, flying low in the Cessna, circling and weaving over the coast to recognize the landmarks in the story and reconstruct *Endeavour*'s course, I was suddenly moved and excited by his tremendous adventure. Here she had come, the Whitby collier, the 'coal cat' from our East coast, un-stoppably pushing her blunt nose into the least-known corners of the seas. *Cape Tribulation* Cook named the headland off which disaster struck him; *Endeavour Reef* the bank of coral on which his ship grounded by moonlight; *Weary Bay* the wide bay they struggled across pumping continuously (seen from the air, it so horribly lacks any refuge); *Hope Island* where they hoped to beach for repairs, but were driven off by the reefs. The coral is everywhere; flying low above the pattern of reefs they are beautiful, shimmering peacock colours fringed with the lace edges of their foam. But when *Endeavour* at last achieved an anchorage in the mouth of the river named after her, beside which Cooktown now stands, and they pulled her up on the high tide and lashed her to an Ironwood tree, they found that what had saved them was a piece of coral which had pierced the hull and then broken off and remained partially blocking the worst hole.

That morning, flying so incongruously in comfort, with even a flask of coffee and a bunch of tiny sweet Canary bananas,

I became a Cook's woman.

We flew on North to Lizard Island where Cook, trying to break out from the Reef to open sea again, climbed the hill for a wider view and saw the gap of clear water which now bears his name, *Cook's Passage*. We landed on Lizard Island, unchanged except for a sand runway, and when we were ready to leave, the engine wouldn't start. It was only an airlock, quite common in small planes when the heat of the sun vaporizes the fuel in the fuel line, and after twenty minutes she took off perfectly. But for perhaps three of those minutes, one realized the appalling helplessness of being alive in that loneliness, shining, moving, alien, empty.

There are ambitious plans to develop Lizard Island!

In the main street of Cooktown is a pub unbelievably like a saloon in any very early Western. On the wall behind the bar is a picture of that same bar painted fifty years ago with five of its habitués in their usual position. Three of them are still there; were actually there when we went in. Not bad! In the cemetery are Chinese graves. 10,000 coolies once worked gold in the Palmer River.

On the coast near where Cook had landed we saw a grove of black and ragged trees growing out of swamp, alive and clamorous with hordes of flying foxes massing in them for the night. You couldn't pick out the individuals once they had alighted, but the trees shivered and screamed with them.

Flying south to Cairns between the coast of Queensland and the Great Barrier Reef, the land is not firm land but mangrove swamp and the mangroves march out into the sea like little groups of bathers. Could there be a more inhospitable coast? The sea is coral and the land is swamp. This continent was not ready to be lived in. Its surface, its animals and birds, its humans, belonged to a remote age not yet fully emerged. This is what all the characters in Russell Drysdale's pictures are looking at – this unanswerable land.

I suppose Canberra had to happen in answer to this. A placed, planned city, made not grown. A remote and insulated capital, segregated from the country it governs. The whole pattern of buildings and water and trees and thoroughfares is a magnificent free use of space. 'We've got it so why not use it?' But the loneliness, the cut-off feeling is here too. Everything under control except the human reaction perhaps? Because people here do feel cut off. 'We're so out of touch here. We want to send our children away to be educated. It's so bad for them to be brought up in a vacuum. This place is an island. How can we know how people feel? What's going on?'

Snugged into the interstices of the university the more conventional professorial characters may look only inwards, but many people look restlessly outwards.

I had heard that no one can visit the war memorial in Canberra and emerge unmoved. Wandering through this vast museum one soon sees why. The memorial is intended to be, and is, a national statement for history. A raw emotion floods the building. It is not sentimental. 'Make no mistake, those men were killers,' an Australian said to us of the men who had gone to the wars. But killers with a vision. The known world had discarded the people who made this race. But a race it has become in a way neither Americans nor Canadians are a race. Something different. The physical continent, their unceasing antagonist, has made them that. Thrown out helpless, they came back in great strength to the old world that had rejected them. This seemed to me the message of the memorial. Details are massed and displayed with an assumption of their importance that makes them the stuff of legend. They speak as clearly as a voice. 'This is how it was – like this – like this.' Paintings of the great convoys setting out from Sydney Harbour in 1914. 'We are coming. Nothing you can bring against us is worse than we have known. Show us our enemy.' Meticulous drawings of the Gallipoli landings (overwhelming to us who had sailed *Mary Deare* through the Dardanelles past those beaches where the two great monuments stand, one to the Anzacs, one to the Turks), showcases of uniforms lovingly preserved: fighting men's, nurses', technicians' with their equipment. Photographs of the animals, giving their unit, their harness. A special showcase for the famous mule who carried so many wounded men up Suvla beach. Records of the Second World War follow so smoothly that it seems one continuous national outpouring. The proportions of the building are superb, culminating in the chapel, the seemingly uncountable list of names according to unit. The miracle is that each one is made to matter, because the people who dreamed this memorial felt that way. This value in everything is the point; and the setting of the whole building in Canberra's vistas of water and trees.

No one had told me how beautiful Australia is. Not a repetition of beauty seen in other countries, mountains, lakes, snow, rivers, forests – but a different, unique beauty of colour and light and space. Driving through New South Wales on a late summer evening (April) the creamy short dead grass rolled endlessly under the clumps of gum trees, the blue-green streamers of the gum trees, whose trunks and branches make patterns against the sky as beautiful as olives or pines. The ghost gums with their silky white bark, drifting in endless variety of twists and curves against the pink earth which is the colour of Australia. Always from now on it seems these colours were around us, red earth, blue-green gums and the white trunks and branches. One seldom loses a distant horizon of low blue hills, really blue, positively blue, not just blue with distance. (Someone suggested the gums covering them give off a resin which thickens the air and this accounts for their being bluer than other hills.) 'Ghost gums' I gathered is an overall name for any eucalypts which have white bark. These are the colours that haunt the palettes of Australian painters – Drysdale, Nolan, Boyd, Juniper.

Driving back from the Snowy Mountains to Cooma there are very dark sheep which exactly match the greyish boulders lying on the ground round there, so it is difficult to tell which is pretending to be which. Swarms of parrots arrive, too swiftly to focus. Only when they have alighted and a tree rustles with red and green can you see them, incessantly moving, incessantly talking, and then with a scream and a swoop they are off again. They strip a branch and move on, so every tree has dead branches sticking up like limbs. On a dead branch hanging over the road on this pink and gold evening we saw an unfamiliar bird. 'A kookaburra' I guessed wildly, and it was! It didn't laugh at us, as they usually do, it didn't make a sound, but nearly twisted its big round head off to see us from different angles. Very unshy birds, they are not alarmed by car doors opening and people getting out, but return the interest with bright eyes and complete poise.

It had been very cold in the Snowy Mountains, as we got out of the car to read the charts explaining the greatest irrigation scheme in the world and to glimpse some of the reservoirs. 'More water than is contained in Sydney Harbour' – I can understand comparisons like that when the figures convey little. We had been lent the key to the Schlink Pass, the highest pass in Australia. The fascinating puzzle padlock, then a roughish road climbing steeply and circling through

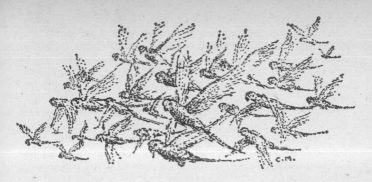

wooded hills. As the ground dropped away from our path
down to the valley, a pair of large black wedge-tailed eagles
sailed past us. The immense pair planed and swooped in
magnificent display against a background of empty sky framed
in bare trees.

The country round Cooma is exiles land, voluntary eager
exiles, but it is still haunted by adventurous Border Scots who
settled there because in some strange way it has the look of
the Border. Great fortunes have been wrung out of it and it
has absorbed people till they could not bear to live anywhere
else. A rich gay life when wool prices were high – remembered
customs adapted to the new space – and beautiful homes were
built. We visited one whose name had been familiar to me all
my life, the home of three generations of my cousins. It was
not here that their grandfather, my grandfather, and a third
brother had settled. That had been in Riverina and the place
where they crossed the Murrumbidgee River is still called by
their name in the old maps, though now a town called Hay
stands there. They first landed at Portland in 1849 and made
their home at Mungadel. They lost their stock to something
then called the coastal disease, known now to have been due
to a vitamin deficiency in the soil, and my grandfather went
west to look for gold to recoup his fortunes, found some, and
came back here to New South Wales to start again.

We stopped so often to look at the early evening vistas of
endless rolling land that by the time we arrived at the house
it was too dark to take a photograph and I cannot remember
it as clearly as I would like. The word 'homestead' is suddenly
so natural and right. You drive on and on, each rise of land,
or grove of trees, each bend of track might hide it; but

no, mile after mile while time passes, on and on, and then at last, suddenly, unbelievably alone, a house, the homestead, approached through trees but facing open country, built on rising ground, a long, low house with a line of very steep and unusual gables. In front, flights of steps and a terraced garden drop to the place where we get out of the car. 'The garden's neglected now, I'm afraid. It used to be pretty.' To one side a long glade peopled with little groups of gums and beyond – distance. 'Isn't that the most beautiful thing you've ever seen?' No, but if it were my home, if I'd grown up there, I, too, would think it was. A wide verandah runs round the house. Our host pacing rangily and restlessly in front of the house to welcome us. Only two people here now.

But I knew them all when they were young. How gay it must have been then at this house whose beautiful name I have heard ever since I can remember! A party before they all came to Europe? A party when they came back? Christmas, Birthdays, Summer dances? Music had poured out of these windows. The newest records, a dance band from Cooma, perhaps? – people. Who had come out with whom on to this verandah on summer nights? And riding out in the early freshness of boundless mornings? They had all been so gay. Now I have seen it.

At this moment the house is under the blow of a tragic accident. And behind that the insoluble problem of falling wool prices and soaring labour costs. A famous homestead on an adjoining station, the land parcelled, had just been withdrawn from sale because there were no offers. *The Cherry Orchard* happens everywhere. But a nice meal is whipped up in a cosy room and a wonderful bottle of wine; the really lovely Australian wine comes from small producers, not the huge combines, and it is all ordered by private customers, so that it is only in the homes of friends you realize how fine it can be. Tragedy has not conquered the hospitality of this house. We sit by the fire among the books and photographs and memories and oddly no sense now of isolation, only of contact, thoughts, ideas, awareness, quick brains very much in touch. Glamorous photographs of a new generation now in their teens, just as gay and of-the-moment as their parents were, making different lives in a different world, but still ambitious, far-ranging, unexpected. (And the beautiful drawing room behind its fly-screen, like an old English country drawing room, its big windows looking down that glade now timeless with moonlight – will it ever be opened, and full, and gay again?)

'Melbourne' was a word I first saw written below my father's signature on the yellowing flyleaves of a few books. This, his handwriting, always seemed the most vivid and personal thing I had of him. Leisurely, luxurious, *old* Melbourne! 'You can't go there,' people in Sydney said, 'the climate'll kill you – it's as bad as England!' Indeed walking through the beautiful gardens among the yellowing leaves of late summer in the April sunshine was just like walking through a London park in October. And here in the gardens is the cottage where James Cook's aunt and uncle lived in Cumberland, his home as a boy. Brought out and re-erected, companioned with trees, and visited, it seems, by a steady stream of people on even the most ordinary working day.

I wallowed in the luxury of the Windsor Hotel where a housemaid lets herself in very quietly, before you are awake, to dust your sittingroom and make sure the flowers are all fresh before you take breakfast there. The good furniture, pictures, clocks, ornaments, the quality of the curtains, the individual private house look, the space, all make the hotel resemble a cross between Claridge's and the old Cavendish in Rosa Lewis's day. How cherished and protected you feel!

We flew to Alice Springs, less to visit that unique tourist resort than to see the great red monoliths, Ayers Rock and the Olgas. And more than either, to turn into the centre of Australia. To see Australia! And not just the occupied sea-board. A great motor road is now complete all round the edge of the continent, but the centre is unknown and savage land into which occasional adventurers make expeditions. Only a few years ago two tribes of aborigines, forced by drought out of their usual territory, emerged far enough to find that white men existed.

Flying over the desert is not monotonous as I had heard. It changes all the time and is fascinating to watch. Looking directly down from the aircraft, you see the red earth between the blades of grass because they are so sparse. But looking ahead or from side to side, the colour of this desert grass merges into a blue-green sea, patched with the silvery salt bushes and the pale gold pincushions of spinifex, streaked with the glitter of dried-up salt lakes, hazed with mirage. The colour of opals.

One is ashamed of flying over it so safely and easily, sharply conscious of what it would be like if the aircraft were a heap of junk on the ground and one saw it all from there, as many have. Endless as the sea, knowing the mirage was not a grove of trees around a waterhole, but something which would move and swirl and dissolve. Knowing the shine was not water, but dried salt. The infinite vast emptiness. Pilots who have flown over it for years said they have never seen any sign of life from the air. All life lies up during the daylight hours under whatever shelter it can find. Early morning and evening are the foraging and feeding times.

The great rocks when at last we reached them are first a blur ahead like tiny clouds, then gradually they become red islands in the blue-green sea. Flying over Ayers Rock is an impertinence; only when you climb part of the way up from the ground and, peering over a shoulder of rock, see its immense slopes and valleys do you get some idea of its bulk. The colour varies with the time of day and the angle of light from flaming crimson to a plummy purple. Walking between the spinifex and the mulga bushes, incessantly brushing the flies off our faces, it is unendurably hot; so that we seek a boring refuge in the comparative cool of the restaurant sitting-room.

From Ayers Rock we were flown out to the Olgas by Harry Purvis, a magnificent-looking old-timer who had flown with Kingsford Smith. The Olgas are a group of rocks equally red, some twenty miles from Ayers Rock, piled up like a castle above the plain. I was studying Harry Purvis's fine profile at the controls when I heard my husband, sitting in front with him – there were just the three of us – say, 'Oh, don't worry about Dorothy, she loves it.' I was just wondering what I was alleged to love when he rolled the plane over and we crawled up the face of the Olgas, then down, and then up again, slowly, very close to the details of the surface. I had never done quite that before and wondered if I should hold together. I did and rather enjoyed it.

I couldn't live in Alice Springs without suffering acute claustrophobia. 'The Alice' is an island surrounded by desert and I should be conscious of the emptiness cutting me off. But the people who live there love the Alice and are proud of her.

The original Alice Springs was built in the 1800s when the telegraph line was put from north to south across the continent. But it is a little apart from the present town, its buildings preserved as a museum full of yellowing photographs of men with black beards, with their camel teams and equipment and relics of their achievement. There really was an Alice and the spring is still there.

The present Alice Springs has a wide main street down which we saw our first aborigines walking with that strange, almost rolling gait – are they always a bit drunk when you see them in towns? Or is it a corruption of the walk that once ate up the miles? Those we saw later in more natural conditions – herding at a sheep-shearing for instance – didn't walk like that. One hates to stare at the strange dark faces – one always hates to stare at people who are different – but in the case of aborigines it is a different fear, difficult to describe. What is one looking at? Something primeval, remote; our ancestors? A journalist in Brisbane had warned us 'not to get involved with this problem'. He had surprised us by producing the subject out of the blue, and had spoken almost with despair.

Alice is full of motels and is a great tourist attraction. Our motel was charming and had a good cook. He was young and ambitious, aiming at variety. At the moment he was going through his Chinese period. I couldn't resist telling him I had been born in Shanghai and he excelled himself. As always in Australia the fact that a place is cut off and everything has to be brought in from far away seems to make it a matter of pride to have a good choice of very fresh food. One is inescapably conscious everywhere that every single thing happens as a result of a battle with conditions, is a victory over conditions. The shellfish he used for his chop-suey were from the Gulf and really tasted of something. The salads, here in the dust and flies and heat, were crisp and copious.

But why the oval plates? This had fascinated me from Dunk Island onwards. Throughout Australia only the very sophisticated restaurants have round plates. 'Why not?' is the obvious answer. 'Why do you have round ones?' But do they really hold more? Do they take up less room on the table? Are they more convenient for arranging a whole meal – the vegetables and the inevitable chips are served with the meat or fish on the same oval plate. Does this go back to pioneer days? There must be a reason. Everyone has forgotten it. I would love to know.

The thing I most wanted to see in Alice Springs was the

School of the Air, a radio network reaching out to children on lonely stations, drawing them in and linking them together. Miss Adelaide Miethke who started it in 1951, had done so from the Alice in a little room, tentatively, feeling her way. What a dream to make come true! And how right that it should start in the Red Centre. Now there are six schools of the air, functioning over the Flying Doctor network. We were invited to the splendid new premises and by great good luck it happened to be the first day of the new term, so when the children were called up, each on his or her individual code number, and came on the air, they were telling the teacher and each other what they had done in their holidays. We sat in a wide passage looking through a glass partition into a room where the young teacher sat at a desk, her head craned forward with the concentration of trying to catch what the children were saying. She wore earphones but the voices also came from a loudspeaker. They were not always clear to me, but she repeated them and summarized them so the other children listening in should miss nothing. As each child came in to her call she seemed to be summoning spirits out of space. This is often their only contact with other children. They form friendships and once a year they come into the Alice for a great get-together and meet for the first time the teacher and each other. Sometimes the flesh-and-blood personality is so different from the familiar voice that problems arise. There is a course of lessons which are posted in for correction and this takes the child up to the age at which he comes in to school. Many lonely stations employ a girl, often a European immigrant, as governess, but often they can't stand the loneliness, so it doesn't last long. Drawings and essays entered for competition are displayed on notice boards at the end of our passageway. But what startles and moves one is something more ghostly, yet more important than education: companionship, making friends, someone to talk to, the only contact with other children.

So at last we came to the West. Western Australia, pronounced 'expendable' in the last war because there was no alternative. If the Japs had invaded how could it have been defended on the tenuous thread of one railway line? Ironically, when we were there at the height of the mineral boom the emphasis had shifted until the West looked like being the tail that wagged the dog.

Perth, the capital, and particularly the port of Fremantle,

still has the air of a frontier town. In Sydney they say the question to ask a stranger is 'How much money do you make?', in Melbourne 'Where did you go to school?', but in Perth 'Where have you come from?' For he must have come either from the remote outer world, or else from the other part of Australia which until very recently seemed equally foreign.

In the North West the earth is a particularly dark, heavy red. Remembering the rich red earth of Devonshire or Virginia I thought this too might be good growing land if only it could be irrigated. But no, it is sterile however much you water it. And if you want to grow anything you must import earth and make a layer on top. This earth grows nothing but money. This is where the iron ore comes from. 'If you're really going to be shown all the processes, you must soak any clothes you've worn in cold water before you send them to the cleaners or laundry,' we were told before we left Perth for Port Dampier and its mining town, Tom Price; Port Hedland and its mining town, Mt Newman. 'The particles of red dust up there are a particular shape, very tenacious. Unless you soak them out first anything you wear will be permanently stained.'

'They've had it hot up there. Shouldn't be bad now (May – autumn). Should be under the hundred now.'

It was under a hundred and people who had come through the summer stood out in the sun chatting and not finding it hot, but I longed to take a couple of cowardly steps into the mercy of shade. The sun here is not a holiday pleasure, but the enemy in spite of which you toil.

The Company towns with their rows of neat little houses are graded according to the rank of the occupants, but all are beautifully designed and equipped (how else could you get people to work there?). Earth is laid and grass seed grown and trees planted and gardens made (how else could people live without some reminder of living things?). The Walkabout Motels built round a courtyard with a swimming pool and trees and flowers shutting out the world are used as clubs for the residents, as well as hotels for visitors. Charming dining-rooms with full and good menus, everything brought up from Perth in refrigerated trucks, fish, meat, vegetables, salads, drink. 'We make it a custom to wear ties in the restaurant in the evening – a matter of morale really.' One's mind leaps back to the British in India – fascinating how the same techniques emerge in the face of similar challenges – this business of keeping yourself going, of making yourself feel on top, of not surrendering to the climate. Always derided by people who have never worked under such conditions. All the pretty young wives at a party they gave for us, so smartly dressed, had had their hair done that morning. I was ashamed that mine felt stiff and was turning faintly auburn with the red dust, though I had worn a double scarf under the regulation safety helmet during the day. We had been shown the sequence of each twenty-four hours' work from the arrival of the iron ore, which had been blasted the previous evening, to its departure in the ship's hold.

There is a strange beauty about powerful machinery in silhouette against space – the monsters of this dark red world – for it is surface mining, and always beyond there is gum tree bluish green country and the golden light.

One evening after dinner we were taken for a drive into the bush to look for kangaroos. We failed to find any, but driving home, Dampier looked rootless as a film set, an invasion, held together by the motive of high, though not excessive, pay for very long hours of work under gruelling conditions. But also by something else. 'It's the beginning that was exciting,' the mine manager's wife said to me – she had been one of the first four wives up there. 'We all sowed our grass patches the same day as soon as they laid some earth and brought us water, and when the first blades came through we rushed to each other's houses to see them. You really did feel like a pioneer. Now it's so big and growing all the time, rivalries creep in and it's become more like any other place.'

But for the visitor there is still an enormous élan, a sheer excitement at the speed and energy and size of the achievement. The port at Dampier was built in nineteen months and a year later was shipping out a larger tonnage than any other port in Australia. Next year there will be more and more. There is the vigour and pride of an assault unit – there has to be. What though a top executive, a Scot, said, 'I sometimes wonder what we are doing – making thousands more cars for people to kill themselves with and filling the world with scrap?' But the giant impetus rolls on. 'What happens when the world doesn't want any more iron ore?' you ask. 'Ah, that's the one thing we don't think about!'

At Mt Newman we saw the blasting. This is the climax of each day's work. All these men in their hard helmets and their clothes soaked with the red dust, their zoo of monster machines, have toiled all day to prepare for destruction the next slice of the diminishing mountain. It is cut across like a cake. Blasting is at six o'clock – the time when the sun is slanting and the light thickens. We withdraw to a little hill, as near as is safe, and slightly to one side. The manager's car in which we sit has inter-car radio and he talks to the head engineer, who at this moment is King, and is the last man to leave the scene prepared for blasting. We see the work teams withdraw leaving their equipment protected. An extraordinary silence grows. Only the brief relevant sentences exchanged on the inter-car radios. Finally, the little white car of the head engineer moves from the plain before the ravaged hill face where now nothing moves at all. He seems to move slowly because his car looks like an insect in the vastness, but in a surprisingly short time he is beside us to watch from this vantage point. Now nothing moves or speaks. The red rock face stands in the evening light, very clear and solid against the pale distance. The explosion we are waiting for comes as a terrifying shock. The rumbling crash lasts so long, growing and fading. An immense cloud of purple dust rises to veil this obscenity of power, but through it you see for an instant the whole cliff face bow and crumble and lie in rubble. The red cloud rises into the clear pale sky in the shape of a dragon and then, a slowly dissolving dragon, moves off over the bush.

The first kangaroo I saw was a dead one. 'And that's all you need to know,' said our companion. 'That is the story.' Those great rounded lumps in the road became familiar. The first one, a young male, was very recently killed and his wife and child were still hovering by him. 'Look, look, the ginny and the joey!' When she saw us she hopped a few feet to the side of the track up on to a little hillock and the joey followed her, but when I looked back they had returned and were again hovering round the body. In a three-hour drive we passed five other rounded lumps in the road in various stages of disintegra-tion – the curve of a kangaroo's body shows up a long way off. They are blinded by the headlights of cars at night and stand still. Switch off to give them an instant of darkness and they

would leap from the track. But the faster you drive a Land-Rover over a dirt road the less you feel the rough surface, so no-one reckons to stop or slow.

We saw a new Company town being laid out in the bush, exactly like a military operation. On the way back we picnicked in a glade of exquisite gum trees. When we'd finished, our hostess picked up the plastic cloth by its four corners and rolled everything in it, paper plates and empty plastic cups and plastic cutlery and uneaten food and folded it all together – rubbish.

At Port Hedland the new mining town is cheek by jowl with the crumbling old town – clapperboard houses and a curiously grey dusty look of disintegration on buildings and people, a faded look of something left over; many aborigines about the streets.

Here in the North West you find the débris of the original Australia that the overwhelming majority of Australians, who live in the cities, never see. But there is a fast growing wave of tourism from the cities to see the country. A thoughtful journalist in Queensland had suggested to us that 'every nation must have something to believe in about itself. With us it's been our record in the two World Wars. But new generations can't live on that for ever – don't want to. The new thing may be pride and interest in the actual physical Australia, the place itself, our fauna, our flora, our birds. A sense that these are unique possessions worth taking care of. Five minutes ago (it seems) conservation was a dirty word. Now! It's at least paid lip service! If we have time . . . ?'

I remembered a very small boy on Heron Island saying to an even smaller boy who was bearing down on a fish, 'No, you're not allowed to kill it.' 'Why not?' 'Because it's a nature reserve.' 'What's that?' 'It means you can't kill anything.'

And I remember another child's voice, one of those coming over the air at Alice Springs telling about their holidays. 'We were driving home from visiting my grandmother and we saw some dingo puppies playing in the road. We couldn't shoot them because we hadn't a gun, but we managed to run over one.'

I found an old picture postcard of two aborigine children sitting on the ground playing with a yellow half-grown dingo. They came to Australia together, the aborigines and their dingoes, at least ten thousand years ago. In the spare nomadic

Aborigine Rock Drawing

life of hunting and foraging, the black people and their dogs moved over Australia through the millenia, with very little interference from the outside world from the days of the Dreamtime until a mere couple of hundred years ago. The Dreamtime is the aborigines' legendary remote past when the gods and goddesses took the form of animals and birds, rocks and trees, and gave people in the form of stories the rules by which to live. From this comes the tremendous importance they attach to certain places and objects – the Word made matter.

Behind the aborigines as we saw them I had a painting by Elizabeth Durack hanging like a backcloth in my mind, for she painted them in the Kimberleys where she had grown up on the vast Durack lands – sixty thousand square miles. There the aborigines could live much as they had always done. This picture that haunts me is still in her possession and dominates her drawing room in Perth. A pearly, open picture of water and rocks and lithe black bodies – four or five different groups of them variously occupied – fishing, cooking, playing with a baby – the camp life of this particular group. 'Can you see a dog painted out in the bottom foreground?' she asked. 'He died while I was working on the picture and they were so upset they thought it was dreadful he should be still in the picture when he wasn't there really, so they made me paint him out.' The picture has an extraordinary freshness, a way of life unchanged from the dawn of the human race. The un-hurried busy-ness of just living; occupiers of the natural world.

'The aborigines live in unbelievable squalor,' a friend said, showing us a recently abandoned abo camp in the bush. The tiny low shelters were made of every conceivable man-made material salvaged from rubbish dumps – corrugated iron, wire, wood, plastic, bits of derelict furniture, newspapers; tins and plastic and beer bottles littered the place. But these materials are miraculous and fascinating in their eyes, a great improvement on the grasses and branches of trees which their ancestors used to construct these little shelters against the heat of the sun. There had been nothing sordid about them!

We were driven through a reserve by an errant secretary who said, 'I don't know that Mr X would like you to see this. So what . . . ?'

But is it worth maintaining life without purpose? These are people. Many are young, what lies ahead of them? One is ashamed to look at the listless extraordinary faces coming to the doors of the huts – a woman stirring a black pot – an elderly man, his hair grey against the black skin, lying stretched out on a narrow bench, turning over and raising himself on his elbow to see who was passing – and farther on, a naked ebony boy standing stretched taut, one hand behind his head, staring at us.

Different people's experiences build up an anthology of despair. 'Yes, I worked with the aborigines. I never thought I'd come to agree with people who say the only hope is to take the children away from them very young and bring them up with us – I thought it was an awful idea. But now I'm not sure it isn't the only thing.' 'I was a nurse up in the Kimberleys among the abos – they're so beautiful, so beautiful!' 'In three generations they breed out – if they marry white people. Strange, isn't it? You know how long most coloured strains persist – but the aboriginal disappears.' The Welfare. The Mission. 'The abos never do anything to help themselves, and do you know how much they cost us?'

'Once there was the Dreamtime.' Early one morning we were taken out into the bush to see the animals. 'If you're interested I'd like to take you to a place I often go to. There's moisture and foliage. Kangaroos rely for water on the dew in the morning. It's a good place. If you just stay still for a bit something generally comes along. But we must be early. That's when they forage, else they'll all have gone to lie-up for the day and you won't see a thing.'

First Bush Turkeys, or Bush Chickens – big, round birds, difficult to believe they're real. Then – oh where? where? why can I never see things in time? But she is standing still – she – the brumbie mare, with a foal beside her. Not really a wild horse, but descended from the horses, many of them Arab, brought to Australia in the mid-nineteenth century – now wild for so many generations. To anyone accustomed only to manhandled-horses, the first sight of a horse that at least believes itself to be wild, born of horses that have lived wild for a hundred years, is extraordinarily moving. So this is what they are really like, not knowing slavery; this rippling grace and beauty, this ease. They are very shy but a closed car always seems accepted by animals. Then the stallion emerged from the trees and came to stand beside her. He was black and glorious. For a moment the unbelievable classic group, unbroken, unspoiled, free, stood looking towards us. Then the stallion shouldered her gently and, putting himself between her and us, moved them away. They flowed into the bush with streaming tails, and vanished.

We cruised gently for a while seeing nothing, then stopped in another place. The bush here seemed golden, perhaps with sunrise. Again I was slow to see them, because they too seemed golden, only the movement shows. Kangaroos. Once I had focused them – and they were quite close – they seemed endless.

Later I was to glimpse many in ones and twos beside dirt roads at dusk and dawn. But this was the only time I felt the richness and profusion of what had been and is now threatened. They poured along, the grace of their leaping, the latent strength, bodies devised to eat up the miles at speed, here in their own bush where they belong, no one knows for how long – but we know they are one of the oldest inhabitants of our earth. An endless procession, whole bunches of them, leaping through the mulga and salt bush and spinifex under the white barked gums. At last nothing moves. It is over.

We had one last glimpse, fractional in the blink of an eye; the shyest of all – and with reason – the dingo. The beautiful red dog self-coloured on the red earth – one moment he was there, then he was gone, slid under a mulga bush.

It was not then our friend told us – how could he? – but later, at night, when we went with a party to the most famous of the dusty, noisy, crowded saloons in the old town for drinking and dancing. He said through the deafening noise of the band, 'You know the dingo is officially vermin? The Government employ aircraft to drop poison bait, especially in gullies where the bitches lie up to whelp. They are such lovely

117

creatures and they die in great agony.'

A few days later: 'I fought that iniquitous law for ten years,' said the owner of one of the stations (once sheep, now cattle) which was not in debt to the Government, had not been forced to sell land, was not eaten-out to a desert, though it had suffered the same drought as its neighbours. He had resisted the temptation to over-stock when prices were high. 'The poison bait wipes out the tiny marsupials as well, all the unique little desert animals. That particular method has been suspended for two years – simply on grounds of expense – I hope it's never restarted. I've got dingoes here – I don't mind them. They do very little harm, and keep down the wild donkeys. Give Nature a chance to keep a balance.' This was a happy station. His daughter rode her camel to round up stock, and he thought the Mission would do better if they gave the aborigine children a pill when they sang a hymn (which they don't understand) and a sweet every time they remembered one of their own tribal songs. 'They're very musical, the aborigines, did you know? But they're forgetting them. I try and encourage the ones who work on my station to remember their own songs.'

We clambered over primeval rocks to see very early aboriginal rock drawings on this station. Men and women, a dingo suckling pups, a kangaroo with a spear in it. As in the Dordogne, the perspective of the larger figures was fantastic, remembering the artist could not see one end of his work when he was drawing the other.

But we sat on another station over a table sticky with spilt beer and buzzing with flies, and the owner said proudly, 'We've been very clever with our vermin control laws – we've carefully worded it so they get the scalp money not only on dingoes but on any dog they bring in – and especially the blacks' dogs!' He sat laughing behind the buzzing flies and said that. Some stations had been so over-stocked when wool prices were high that now they were brown, not with brown grass but with brown earth, bare.

It was left for a TV cameraman in Perth to tell us about the most authoritative book on the dingo. Written by an ex-dogger, Sid Wright, who after years of pursuing and studying dingoes in order to kill them, became so impressed by the character and behaviour of the breed, their mating selection rituals, their life-long partnerships – that he put all he had learned about them into *The Way of the Dingo*, in an effort to quash the mistaken ideas which are used as excuses to exterminate this unique species.

We visited briefly another station where the owner spoke of 'dealing with twenty camels before breakfast'.

It was rare to pick up a newspaper in any part of Australia at this time without seeing the word kangaroo in headlines. 'No species could survive the mass slaughter of the mobile meat factories.' A documentary film on TV showed their methods. 'Each female killed means the death of four – the young in the pouch, the young in the womb, the young who is running but still dependent.' The Central Government in Canberra, it was stated, has never received so many representations on any other single subject. Day after day debates and questions – on one side the bitter irreversible facts of massacre and threatened extermination. On the other, the Minister of Agriculture stone-walling because the export of kangaroo meat brought in revenue.

It was Conservation Year, 1970.

I remember a morning when such a wave of despair overcame me, of grief for the original families of Australia – the aborigines and their dingoes, the kangaroos, that I could barely drag up the energy to put my possessions into the suitcases.

We bumped over the red dirt roads, rippling with mirage of water, to Nullagine. I'd longed to know what a hotel called the Conglomerate could be like. It had been a rough drivers' pull-in and a byword for discomfort, but now it was being re-made by a charming couple with great energy – for was not the mineral boom going to transform this area? She insisted on giving us nice sandwiches with our beer at three o'clock in the afternoon, though we'd concealed the fact that we had not fed. Our bedroom was a unit set down on the red earth a little way from the hotel, and not yet finished, but they kindly ran out a cable so we had light, and put mats below the steps so that we didn't walk too much red dust into our room. They lit a fire under an oil drum to heat water in the outside wash house of the hotel, so I had a real bath.

That night when we left the crowded bar to go to our room, hesitating outside in the sudden dark, an aborigine came towards us – that black face, from the unimaginable past of our species, materializing out of the darkness, coming towards us to speak in a strange tongue, holding out his hands. Begging, unknown among them before the white men came, as thieving was unknown in their natural past – now ubiquitous, so compulsively fascinating are even the trashiest manufactured objects. I did not find him frightening in the sense of any menace to us. But terrifying in the sense of what had happened to him, and his race, and what would happen now.

Next morning we bought a handful of rough amethysts from the lady who ran the general store and polished – 'tumbled' – them in her spare time, among the cabbages and tinned food.

From Nullagine we drove out to visit a mine which we like to think of as our personal treasure trove – Blue Spec. Once they'd tried to get the antimony out of the gold, which was very expensive, so the workings were abandoned. Now it may be worth trying to get the gold out of the antimony. We drove through red country with sparse scrub and many outcrops of white quartz, on the edge of the Great Sandy Desert. Finding a few shacks set down in the middle of nowhere, we enquired for the manager, and were directed to a small caravan. We walked to it through shimmering heat, each accompanied by our personal cloud of flies, and knocked at the door. When he came we realized we had woken him from a well-deserved siesta. In spite of this he welcomed us most kindly, and sitting on the side of a bunk with my neck crooked by the one above, I listened to the talk I was later to hear reverently discussed in the financial papers. He was a Yorkshire man who had prospected in many parts of the world. Outside, two rather scarecrow figures were letting a third man down a hole in the ground in a bucket. That was all. It fascinated me, a few months later, to see this place headlined in the City pages. The excitement in the world's capitals – the reality on the spot.

At Marble Bar, 'the hottest place in Australia', the hotel is called the Ironclad, but it is much kinder than it sounds – the usual adequate little motel bedroom, the blinds sealed, the complete meals on an oval plate, always the bottle of pleasant wine and a salad. At Marble Bar itself a few miles away, a river flows below great cliffs among trees, its rocks fantastically veined and seamed and patterned with lovely colours. One feels an inevitable haunting of many presences in this water-hole to which men and animals must have been drawn through the millenia.

From this heat we plunged down, again via Perth, to Albany, in the extreme south-west of Australia. This is the green agricultural place where the wild flowers blaze in the spring. Stopping beside the road to watch a ballet of black swans moving up a little estuary we found on returning to the car that we had parked beside a post with a notice on it, 'POISON', and underneath a statement that poison had been distributed in that vicinity. Fishing and hunting were prohibited. One looked round at the concealing landscape of hedge and trees and bush wondering where the poison bait lay and what creatures would chance upon that nice surprise meal, that agonizing death.

We walked in a grey cathedral of the giant karri tree trunks, the tallest trees in the world, and stood on the rocks of the farthest point of Australia where the Southern ocean beats up from Antarctica over a wild coast of spray and shining rocks and blowholes like Cornwall. In Albany there is now a restaurant in the Old Post Office, rather an impressive building, candle-lit and cosy. It is run by a Dutchman who includes Indonesian dishes in the menu.

Our last foray was to turn inland from Perth and fly to the old gold country. Autumn was here and the weather changing. Kalgoorlie was the goldrush town of the last century. Here my grandfather had come round by ship from New South Wales to recoup his fortunes. He did find gold, and returned to New South Wales to buy land in the fabulous Riverina, where the longest fleeces grow. He and his brothers had a very big holding even by the standards of that time and place. But my grandfather sold his share for a song to go and fight for Garibaldi, whose friend he became and from whom he had many letters. Which he lost, of course.

Here the bearded men with their camel trains had prospected and dug and washed the gold. Here the water supply still comes through a single pipe from Perth, 375 miles away. For many years the Golden Mile has been a line of derelict and abandoned buildings. But now again men crowd the Palace Bar to exchange tips and talk of fortunes. This time it is nickel.

The approach road into Kalgoorlie from the airport passes the famous open brothels – much in the news at this moment because application for licence by a third Madame had pushed even money out of the Kalgoorlie headlines. Glancing through one wide open door I remember a girl in a long white dress, and through another a girl in a long red dress, both standing still, looking out of the doors; just standing, with a kind of passive timelessness.

The main street of Kalgoorlie is wide, built for camel trains. The central crossroads is cornered by wooden buildings of such period perfection one can't bear them to be destroyed and replaced by modern ones, as is threatened.

The Palace Hotel is arguably the most colourful hotel in which I have ever stayed – few hotels have continued to receive guests with so little change from such wild early days. Yes, it is modernized, electricity, bathrooms, the famous bar is no longer as long as it was, part of it being cut off to make another dining room. (There was a Yugo-Slav chef, a dark, enormous man, who sometimes introduced exotica, such as a lovely aubergine paté, correctly labelled *Melanzana & Garlic*, with as an after-thought the warning: *Bred-fruit and Garlic – Very Hot*.) But the main staircase still curves up under the figure like a little Statue of Liberty holding aloft the light, and the furniture, the dim reds and dark greens of walls and upholstery, are solid well-worn Victorian; pleasant maids bring cups of morning tea along endless corridors. The tight groups of excitedly-talking men filling the bar are again prospectors. The few women are kept supplied with drinks, but sit passively, not listening. The pub on the opposite corner has beautiful cut-glass windows like the old London pubs.

The weather grew surprisingly cold, with heavy cloud. Rain made most airfields in West Australia unusable, and floods made some roads impassable. I had not realized that drought country is also flood country – the ground cannot absorb. I had been excited to be invited to visit Poseidon (the first woman, I believe). But we were grounded by low cloud and the expedition could not take place. We felt the sudden claustrophobia of the trapped, the place we had come to so eagerly suddenly a prison. Kalgoorlie was full of people desperately trying to get out, back to Perth.

A New Zealander, ex-test-pilot, now training young pilots on small bush planes, came early in the morning to our bedroom at the Palace and said he'd send a car shortly to bring us to the airfield, and he 'thought it would be all right'.

The airstrip was deserted. Picking our way through the mud, we saw sitting on the step of the single building (waiting-room cum office) a large beautiful pearl-grey dog with pricked ears and curious intelligent pale eyes. There was an indefinable air of the wild about him, a hair-spring alertness, a loneliness, though he sat there with perfect composure.

'H'mm, a touch of the dingo, I think,' our friend said. 'He must belong to one of the pilots.'

On the deserted airstrip there was a tiny plane to take us,

we hoped, to Perth. Our luggage got in, we got in, not till the pilot got in did I believe we were really away.

So much to remember across that continent of contrasts. But it is the original families that leap at me first out of the word Australia. The mangrove trees marching out into the sea off the North Queensland coast; the white-haired aborigine lifting himself on one elbow on his narrow bench and rolling over to look at us, and the naked staring black boy. The golden kangaroos leaping with such strong grace through the golden bush in the early morning light, and the strange pale eyes of the dingo blood lifted to us as the plane rose above Kalgoorlie, cutting us off with severance sharp as a knife from all below, while we flew up and out and on and on over the endless opal-coloured land.

Aborigine Message Sticks

Of course, all this can turn sour, this food business. If you stay a little too late at your favourite restaurant, and a waiter suddenly arrives with your coat, and you realize the cloak-room woman has left to catch the last bus home to her ailing husband. You picture her huddled in a corner, cramped and half asleep, jolting through the diminishing streets.

The lines of tiredness are showing through their professional smiles as the waiters see their customers off, and the customers, with their surfeited, pitiless faces, are they beginning to wonder about their livers, and the scales tomorrow morning?

The man at the only other occupied table is paying now, a great wadge of banknotes pushed out from an elegant cuff. Because he was in your line of vision you have noticed him – the expensive suit a little taut over the slightly plump shoulders as he leaned forward; a cold, too-remote predator stooping over his prey. You remember the frightened eyes of the cattle glimpsed through the slats of the truck bringing them into the city, to the slaughter yards. The sudden thought of soft coats and warm breathing. Rows and rows of calves in the tiny boxes they live in, and suddenly remembering a spring evening in Corsica, when first one and then another cow with her calf beside her, had gathered on a grass slope between trees, until there were five families, and the cows grazed while the calves played – confronting each other in classic, head-on profile, then darting away in the fey wildness that takes young animals at dusk, then prancing off until, afraid of being lost, they rush back to mother and suckle furiously. Trout that never leapt in a brown stream, but came via the deep-freeze from a Danish tank farm. Did I really let anyone pay so much for out-of-season strawberries that had to have cream and liqueur to make them interesting?

We are too far away, too far, we have lost connection. It does not need the reductio ad absurdum of an expensive meal (rushing to the cloakroom to sick it up, more likely nerves than greed) to make one wonder. To make one think with sudden freshness about picking strawberries in June, doubled under the net that spoil's one's hair, too hot because strawberries are always planted where it's warmest, and summer all around. Or running up from the garden with a trug full of aubergines and peppers and tomatoes and onions to the kitchen to make a ratatouille with the late sun slanting redly through the window. Memorable, long-known faces between the Georgian candlesticks; memorable talk, and on the table bottles of beautiful wine, and food for which nothing has suffered and died.

PART IV

SAILING

INTRODUCTION

Meals taken ashore when you are sailing fall into a different category. Even when the restaurant is fine and famous enough to provide an event in itself, the occasion has added glamour because one seems to have come from a different world – in fact has come from a different world. More often, however, particularly in the Greek islands, you sail to some tiny fishing village, or anchor in a bay where there are no buildings, and climb a mule track to reach a village, and encourage someone to cook you a little meal.

'Rude to be so Late' is a tribute to the loved French coast where I did my first sailing.

The record 'Eating Ashore' is a mish-mash of remembered meals, many of them in places you could not reach except under your own sail.

The last piece is added diffidently. It is quite separate – my Galley. Cooking at sea has been an important part of my life, first on *Triune of Troy* and then for ten seasons on *Mary Deare*. Here, as always, the point is in the contrasts. One night there is so much movement on the boat that everything gets up and hits you, and great seas go roaring past the port-hole; you manage to prepare sandwiches and beef tea or soup, and get the food safely into the cold wet hands of tired men in oil-skins, every movement a calculated manoeuvre. The next night you sit at leisure over a nice meal with wine and flowers and candles on the table, while the ship skims fast over the sea, so smoothly that, below, one forgets she is moving.

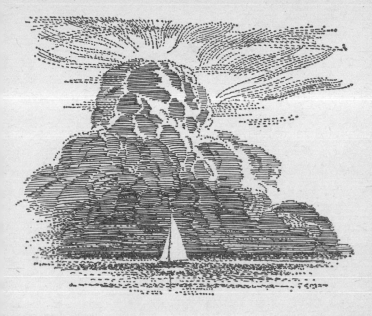

Oh, the shellfish round the Brittany coasts! Haunted by Samuel
Beckett's terrible short story, I still eat lobster. They are
tourist-bait, of course, seldom eaten by local people, who
would regard it as eating good money, but sent alive to the
nearest tourist centre, where they are described as being
straight from the sea – which is true if you count a *vivoir*.
In consequence they seem to be roughly the same high price
everywhere, round Cornwall, the ports of the Bay of Biscay,
all round the Mediterranean, and (allowing for the overheads
of · individual restaurants) in London or Paris or Montreal.
Even if you can bring yourself to buy them from the fisher-
men who so often hold them up squirming beside your boat,
and are prepared to live (as I am not) with the long death
struggle of the creature with protruding eyes crashing about
in the boiling pot, the difference in price is often surprisingly
small.

At Concarneau, Mère Armande was the place. Mère Armande
has retired now, and lives down the quay from the restaurant
which still bears her name, but I remember a night when she
was still there, welcoming, suggesting, serving. Everything went
wrong that night (except the dinner, of course). We'd had a
fairly rough passage up from Spain, and several nights at sea,
so achieving the sanctuary of port meant relaxing over a

lovely meal on shore, and then a long, quiet night's sleep in our bunks.

But we arrived later in the afternoon than we had hoped, and this meant the outer harbour was full, and anyhow we had to water first, and this meant waiting in a long queue of fishing boats at the water-point in the Inner Harbour. A sailing boat, with the windage of her mast and rigging, and her more limited engine, her slender hull and deep draft, is always vulnerable among heavy, shallow motor boats driven like cars.

I was holding a fender ('bumper' or sausage-shaped pad to prevent one boat scraping another) when I realized a fisherman sitting high above me on his deck, was staring straight down the front of my sweater. I could neither change the position of my arm nor call someone else to hold the fender – they'd have said 'What's the matter?' and what could I scream above the hubbub of the harbour down the length of the ship? They'd only have laughed. Besides, as all the boats were moving all the time, I had to move the fender from moment to moment instead of tying it on as usual. So I tried to distract my fisherman with conversation, and we had a nice chat as our two boats slowly moved up to the water-point – about the sardine shoals, the weather, the Pernod. I daren't even look up at him for fear of scraping the boats. The fishers are always afraid of their lovely paint being scratched by the guard-rails of yachts, and he was fending ours off with one foot, having removed his sea-boot so as to do it gently. His toes in the thick stocking curled round it like a hand.

In the midst of all this a very English voice hailed us from a dinghy, inviting us for drinks that evening. As his boat was moored in the outer harbour, we realized he had rowed a long way to find us, after seeing us sail in. Impossible to refuse such a charming gesture.

At last we were watered, found ourselves a mooring, cleaned ourselves up and changed, and rowed ashore through the beautiful coloured sardine fleet riding gently at anchor (less trouble to row than to mount the outboard motor, only to stow it again the next morning before going to sea).

We ordered a bottle of Muscadet to give us strength to choose our dinner, and Mère Armande brought, un-asked, a dish of prawns. *'Pour s'amuser seulement, pour passer le temps.'* They were quite an expensive way of passing the time, I remember.

We ordered hot lobster and I drank Muscadet to forget

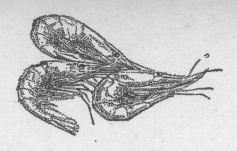

Samuel Beckett's story *Dante and the Lobster*, and what was going on in the kitchen. *She caught up the lobster and laid it on its back. It trembled. 'They feel nothing' she said. For hours, in the midst of its enemies, it had breathed secretly . . . Now it was going alive into scalding water. It had to. Take into the air my quiet breath . . . 'Well,' thought Belacqua, it's a quick death, God help us all. It is not.*

One bottle doesn't last long between four tired people. A new one came with the food, which was perfect. We had wood strawberries to follow. Coffee . . . Lobster does take time, but we were shocked when we looked at our watches. 'What time did they ask us for drinks?' 'Oh, just . . . after dinner.' Time seemed something amenable, under control.

Now that it was dark the quay of shops and restaurants was dominated by the bulk of the old city opposite. The great grey stone arch beckoned us with mystery. It would be wrong to let our friends, who didn't know Concarneau, miss just a glimpse inside. We wandered through the medieval night, remembering the splendid chosen places, looking through the stone slits to the lit harbour. 'We must go back, we shall be disgracefully late,' we kept saying. 'We'll row very hard, it isn't far,' said Richard, who was very tall, very big, his supernormal strength used as gently as a Newfoundland dog's. (When he dressed on board, his head and shoulders stuck up through the forward hatch, so he could give us a running commentary on the life of the harbour.)

But when we arrived back on the beach where we had left the dinghy, no glint of water showed. We had allowed, of course, for the extreme drop of the Brittany tide, mooring the dinghy with plenty of slack. But who were these weird sisters, these huge wooden bottoms we stared up at? — the sardine boats, rounded hull nestling against rounded hull like fat women gossiping, and our little dinghy high and dry among the seaweed, fish bones and garbage of the beach. 'Don't worry,' said Richard. 'We'll make a way through, somehow.' We carried the dinghy over the slimy pebbles and looked up at the impassable barricade of great wooden hulls lolling gently with the movement of the water, just afloat, their positions judged to a nicety by a lifetime of experience. They were two and in some places three deep. Then we heard a snore, very close, and realized the crews were sleeping on board, leaving their boats to go down with the falling tide, and then be re-floated in time to take them to sea in the morning.

'I think I can push them apart,' said Richard, and raised one hand to the curve of the nearest hull. He pushed. Nothing happened. This surprised him; things always moved when he pushed them. 'They're solid as a town,' we told him. 'But they're afloat,' he persisted, 'things move very easily in water, you could almost push the Queen Mary – .' He lifted his other hand to the next sardiner and tried to push them apart, braced, like a young Hercules, exerting for once all his vast strength. A new snore we weren't expecting came from the second ship, as if called forth by Richard's touch. We felt we should whisper as people were sleeping, but we timed it wrong for the snores and had to keep saying 'What?' to each other, while our feet sank in the dredging shingle. 'It's no good, Richard, even if you shifted one, there are others beyond, we'd never open up a gap big enough to get the dinghy through,' Ralph said.

Richard was puzzled, he wasn't used to being defied by inanimate objects. He reached up to enormous height, grasped the stern and scrambled up on board the vessel, and padded off out of our sight. A man checked in mid-snore and we were afraid he'd wake, and surface with a sailor's vigilance to find Richard looming on his deck. 'Richard, come back,' we hissed in warning whispers. He reappeared. 'I can carry the dinghy across the decks of all the sardiners,' he said. 'Can you man-handle it up to me? – then I can help you up and we can launch it on the other side. It's quite easy to step from one to the other.'

'No,' said Ralph. 'These men are tired. We couldn't possibly do that without waking at least two ships' companies, and I know how I'd feel if it were me. Besides, I doubt if it's possible in the dark.' Richard came down, sadly. 'I should be able to move something,' he said. 'Please let me try once more.' The snores were calm and rhythmical again, then a third started, sharper, more querulous. 'That one sounds semi-conscious. Come away, we'll just have to carry the dinghy round to another part of the harbour.'

'Shall we carry Dorothy in the dinghy to keep her feet dry?' asked Richard, always kind.

'No, thank you, I'll go first with the torch, so you don't slip on the steps that are covered with seaweed.' The big torches always seem on board when crises happen ashore, so I've learned to keep a little one in my handbag.

They lifted the dinghy and carried her up to the quay and round to a place where steps went down, and we found water, blessed black rippling water, and floated her. But we had to row right round the two harbours to reach our friends. 'It's too late,' we said. 'Let's go home and sleep, it's only half the distance to *Mary Deare*.' 'We can't, they'll wait up for us. We can explain.' 'Can we?'

The great harbour full of boats was beautiful and utterly silent. Nothing moved but us, skimming through the sleeping boats. Our spirits rose. The Muscadet sparkled in our veins. We had conquered, we had found a bit of sea to put our boat in, the night was ours. Resisting the temptation to hail the dark and silent yachts, we sang softly, and made a rhythm for the oars of the three different snores of the sardine fishers, reproduced as part-song. At last we reached the boat to which we had been bidden. A faint glimmer still showed on board. They were on deck to welcome us. A tiny ship, oil-lit. The cabin was pure period – 'Riddle of the Sands'. Our host and his crew were both young, good-looking, with exquisite manners. They behaved as if we had arrived three hours earlier. We took off our filthy shoes, apologized and tried to explain. They ignored this, sat us down and poured wine. I had an extraordinary sensation of going back in time to the sailing ships of a bygone age. Was this real? – the oil lamps, the silence of the harbour, the lost sense of time. We made a last effort to explain, 'As the tide fell – while we were ashore – the sardine fleet moved down with it till they were all resting together. We couldn't launch the dinghy.' I talked to stop myself from giggling. 'Richard tried to move the fleet with his bare hands, we were so worried about being late . . .' Again they ignored this and talked politely of other things.

I was very sleepy. I remembered the endless row to get back to *Mary Deare*, to my bunk, my pyjamas, my blissful pillow. It was three nights since we had been able to undress and sleep in our bunks. I rose. 'We must go. Please forgive us for keeping you up so late.' We went up on deck. The harbour and the painted ships might have been wrapped in sleep for a hundred years. They said goodbye as if it had been the most normal visit in the world. They were impeccable. But they didn't believe us.

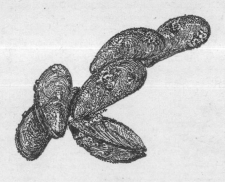

When we sailed in cold seas I felt that dining ashore, and
returning on board at the end of the evening, was the crossing
of a divide. Especially round Normandy and Brittany, where
the sea is a stark neighbour to the wonderful eating places at
the end of the long black-toothed estuaries and the blinding
mists. Here we all were, clean and tidy, with short nails and
seaweed on our shoes, our faces burning a little from wind and
salt, relaxing over the Muscadet and shellfish like everyone else
in the pleasant holiday places. But after? I would look round
at the other tables and think; now we are one of you, sharing
this comfortable room decorated with fishnets and shells, looking out through plate-glass windows at weather and water –
but always, like migrants, a little restless between two worlds,
with half-an-eye for which way a flag is flying; if the slop of
the tide against the beach is more or less; listening for the
wind when the voices are quiet or the door opens. And when
the lights begin to go out you will go upstairs and sleep in
your beds, four strong walls under a steady roof, but we shall
go down to the cruel sea. Over the cobbles of quiet, steep little
streets, then the quay gets slippery and water moves, shining,
in the dark, and there is our dinghy resting safely, oars and
rowlocks neatly stowed. Step down carefully, see if the seat is

wet; everyone in, push off. Now the town we have been part of for a few hours is severed from us irrevocably. Nothing anyone can do for us now, we are on our own. Where is *Mary Deare*? Generally we row straight for our riding light hung in the rigging, but I remember a night in l'Aberwrac'h and one in West Mersea when we rowed into mist, taking our direction from the shore and just hoping, and the lovely line of *Mary Deare* formed gradually in the haze, suddenly looking very big when you're close to her, as a well-designed boat should, but small and compact from a distance, because of the way good lines come together (and a badly designed boat just the opposite, seeming larger than she is from a distance, diminished when you reach her). Our riding light is suddenly above us like a low fuzzy star. Swing up on board, I go first because I carry the key. Fumble for it in my bag, unlock the door, push the bolts of the opposite door, stiff sometimes, push back the hatch, switch on the lights. Home again – the coloured cushions, the familiar books, the chart which had brought us in still on the chart table, and the last entry in the log the time at which we put our anchor down.

A bed-time brandy perhaps? Glasses on the table – goblets below, plastic on deck for fear of broken glass. Over drinks, get out the next chart and study it. Where shall we go tomorrow? Listen to the weather forecast, consider the wind. We have turned from the shore and are looking outward. We have crossed the divide and are Mermen again.

But when we had sailed down to the Mediterranean, this sense of division blurred. Greece, especially, lives on the water as much as on the land, the fireflies spark out to us as we lie at anchor, we can hear the frogs croaking ashore. And a sailing boat tied up at the quay is as much a part of the town as its houses. Over the centuries, boats have been the traffic of these Islands, they were here before the houses, taking people and animals and vegetables from island to island.

These are the occupied seas; treacherous and dangerous with their swift violent squalls, unbearably beautiful with the cool coming of light at dawn or its rich, surfeited withdrawal at evening; or by moonlight, or even in the long colourless haze of noon. But they are peopled seas, more I think than any other seas in the world. The five long summers we sailed them, we had them to ourselves to such an extent that if we saw another craft of any kind we reached for the binoculars to inspect it – yet they are peopled seas. The domestic traffic, as

we see it now, has developed from the domestic traffic of the ancient world – and changed so slowly. In 1965, the women on the smaller Ionian islands were still wearing lovely bunched woollen dresses identical in line with those in the old frescoes, and still drawing water from very ancient wells; but three years later I did not see these dresses. And everywhere stir the legendary heroes who sailed for Troy and the gods who harassed them – not mythical at all when you are sailing their seas in a boat about the size of theirs. The same coasts offer the same hazards, tides and winds are so localized that their personification of the elements into most unreliable gods and goddesses becomes a commonplace of our own sailing, their despairs and delights our own. And behind the tumult of the Homeric days, looking back down an endless tunnel of time, there is Theseus flying from the cataclysm of Crete, leaving lovely drunken Ariadne on Naxos with the wine-god; Phaedra gazing always towards Troezen, and the long shore where Hippolytus and his chariot and horses were dashed to pieces by a tidal wave. And behind them again – so far off one remembers with almost a shiver of distance – that ship for whom surely these seas were really empty, unknown and perilous, Jason and Medea pushing the Golden Fleece ahead of her pursuers. Empty, crowded, living Greek seas.

We ate red mullet. I often wondered how so many conversations in different places all achieved the same little fishes. Could we never learn it would all be the same in the end?

The glimmering cool of evening as we row ashore is part of these meals, then the welcome as the patron bustles out with a little table. Always it needs something under one leg to keep it steady on the uneven ground, and as there are always a sprinkling of bottle tops lying around we just search the ground and pick one like a daisy. The *meze* comes first – usually black olives and the soft white cheese *feta* and bread – bread that tastes of something, and no wonder. Seeking bread to take to sea, you could find the bakery in a small town by just following your nose, sniffing the trail of crusty fresh-baked loaves. For the *meze* it is meticulously cut into neat little cubes. Then the retsina. Now we feel better, and can relax. We have stopped. Now we can consider the next event.

The idea of giving us a meal generally seems rather a shock. I think our clothes and language and *Mary Deare* dreaming at anchor in the bay, make them fear we want elaborate mysteries such as tourist hotels offer. We would lead the conversation to fish, and their faces would light up. '*Psari! Nay, nay*,' (the affirmative that sounds so odd to us). We would all go to the kitchen and explore the fridge. Whoever the commercial travellers were who first took refrigerators by boat and mule through the Greek islands, they deserve to be remembered beside the earlier legend – that African explorers breaking into new country always met the Singer Sewing Machine salesman coming back.

The fattest red mullets would be picked out, and the numbers decided. Then the turning gesture of the hand to explain we wanted them grilled and not fried. Then back to our table, the battle won, the second bottle of retsina poured. I was disappointed to find that only in the Aegean and the Peloponnese is retsina the local wine, on draught in variety from dark to light, so you can taste your way round the barrels in the wine shop and have your own bottles filled up with the one you like best. In the Dodecanese and in the Ionian isles you must order it in bottles – or unresinated wine if you prefer. We found Paulina or Santa Helena the best of the unresinated. As to when and why the Greeks started resinating their wine – this is something oenologists argue over happily. My favourite story is that during the endless Greco-Turkish wars the Greeks, abandoning a position in haste, wanted to spoil the wine they couldn't take with them to prevent the Turks from enjoying it, so they poured resin into the barrels. But later they re-took the position, and having nothing else to drink, tried the wine they had resinated and found it surprisingly good. We realized that resin kills the fermentation of very young wine, so that one can drink it in considerable quantities with no ill effects. In the Ionian, on the other hand, the local draught wine is so fermented that we thought at first it was some kind of cider.

Racing up through the pinewoods on Aegina the night we sailed into Ayia Marina Bay, trying to reach, before the light faded, the great Doric Temple we had seen from the sea, and failing, and being rewarded instead by a distant glimmer of the lights of Athens (for me the first sight of the flame-bright City) we saw, stumbling down over the pine-roots in the sweet-smelling dark, all the little tin cups fixed to the trunks of the pine trees to catch the resin for the wine. I thought, 'This isn't just any wood. This is a Greek wood. I am walking through a strong and ancient magic. Very old powers stir here.' And at the bottom, the first of these meals which have blurred in my mind to one meal, lingered over against an endless pageant of Greek dusks. Always the same sequence : the rickety table, the bottle stopper to steady it, the *meze*, the wine. Then the knives and forks wrapped in a paper serviette, the bread, the beautiful spring water in the newly-rinsed glasses, the salad of tomato and cucumber. The red mullet. The sauce of ripe lemon juice and freshly pressed olive oil.

Yet some stand out, whole and complete, never to be blurred or forgotten. Such a one is our first night on Kythnos during our last season in Greek waters. The single line of little houses seemed lonely under a wild sky. There was only one table in the kafeníon, and four men were playing cards on it, so we withdrew, apologizing. But that morning, setting out to walk endless hot winding miles to the other end of the island, we had had the luck to intercept a lobster before they took him away by boat to the nearest restaurant. So they were expecting us – indeed had seen us leave *Mary Deare* in the dinghy and row ashore – and insisted on moving to finish the game on the counter, first carrying the table out and setting it on the edge of the quay. To our left was the curve of the shore, to our right the rocks of the estuary running out to sea, and a profligate overturned paint-box of colours dazzled over the whole sky and water, leaving one abandoned on the cooling, colourless earth. Behind us, between our table and the kafeníon, passed a procession in silent, unexpected groups, of men and girls and donkeys, half-hidden in great loads of long grass they had just cut from the fields for their animals. One heard the swish and slither of the fresh green grass before the soft pad of feet. Oh, lobster and retsina and the cool breeze just stirring round our lonely little table set flimsily on the edge of the sea, and *Mary Deare* alone in the bay, seeming to be always gliding forward because of the shining ripples moving past her, and over us the almost frightening splendour of the changing sky! This of all meals is a meal to remember.

The second night we ate red mullet.

I only remember one other lobster in Greek shoregoings – apart of course from the big places like Corfu and Rhodes and Mykonos and Hydra, where there is everything, but then so there is at home. But at Serifos, when we went ashore at Limini Livadhi, an old man came to us as we lifted the dinghy ashore, and insisted on taking us along to his cottage, making pincer gestures, so we should know where to eat. But first this great entrepreneur introduced his son, who had the taxi. Not *a* taxi. The first and only taxi on the island. We should go up to the Chora to see the view, then come down and eat the lobster. This seemed an un-improvable programme. After the hooting, triumphant progress of the taxi through the admiring populace, we roared (if this elderly but still spirited vehicle could be said to roar) up endless hairpin bends to the village at the top, and looked down over slopes that seemed lush and green to us after the Dry Islands.

Our host's wife and daughters and some other relations had gathered to welcome us back from this adventure, and we sat in the little garden behind their house in a tangle of flowers and herbs. They picked wild, scented bunches of them for us to take back on board, while he beat up the lobster coral and brains into oil and lemon juice, the sweet flavourful lemons ripened on the tree, with the priest-like devotion of the real cook. He picked a dish of herbs for salad of which I could never find the name – small thin leaves rather like Lamb's Delight, but quite different in taste; aromatic, faintly pungent.

The table was laid in their sitting room among the family photographs – a boy in Greek army uniform, another who had gone to Australia, and women, Byron's dark-eyed fertile women inside their prim black best dresses with lockets at their throats. When all was ready, he ushered us into the lamp-light from the dark garden with a sense of occasion the Tour

d'Argent and Claridge's and the Four Seasons put together could not have excelled. Nor could they have served anything more perfect.

There is a row of deciduous trees along the shore at Limini Livadhi, round dark little trees against the curve of low white houses, and when we were back on board they were full of nightingales singing against the croaking of frogs and the long blurred note of the cicadas – all singing because the moon was so bright.

At Sifnos, the last of the Turkish Delight towns, the boats tie up on a wide and busy quay of shops and cafés, and the restaurant opposite us surprised us by bringing a table across the road and putting it just at the other end of our little gangplank, and serving us there, so boat and town were truly linked.

At Skala Oreos, facing the mainland from the north of Euboea, a row of fiercely competitive restaurants all offer the same food, their grilled and skewered meats and fishes all turning and smoking and sizzling for attention, so you can walk along and compare. For more pleasing décor the tables are set on the other side of the road, under the pepper trees beside the sea wall, and our waiter ran back and forth balancing unbelievable quantities of dishes and plates and bottles, dodging between cars, never dropping or spilling anything in all the time we watched him. You would never think a man could run so fast carrying so many dishes. He was one of the very few waiters who really cared about things being hot. I think he must have enjoyed the excitement of playing it as a danger game. Perhaps he was just determined to beat the other restaurants on either side.

Sometimes the lordly dentice came our way – the first time when we were stormbound under Sounion (strange to be storm-bound with a blue sky and bright hot sunshine! but the

sea was a tumult of whitecaps). We'd been for a long walk to examine the famous monument at close quarters, but surely it is only from the sea that you can understand Sounion, the immense temple which was the last glimpse of their homeland to the early Greek seamen setting out for the Ionian colonies, or the mysterious West? Huge, high, beautiful, it glimmers for so long as you sail away, memory keeps it in the sky when at last it has faded. When we came back, hungry, to the restaurant down by the shore where we had ordered lunch, we expected two or three small dentici, as there were five of us, and were a little cross at having to wait so long. But when it came! – with the bustle of excitement that makes small Greek restaurants such fun, there on a huge dish reposed one magnificent dentice, ample for us all, its head displaying the teeth for which it is named, garnished with lemon halves and cooked to perfection. Never again did I see such a dentice.

But another year, far away in the Ionian at Gayo on Paxos, two dentici were nearly our undoing. Gayo is the prettiest of all the ports, like a set for an opera bouffe. Perhaps it is the red-painted Irma-la-Douce lampstandards that make it look so lighthearted? And at night a man comes round and lights each individual oil-lamp. The first time we came to Gayo – heart in mouth through the narrow entrance, with houses high above us coating the steep hill, until suddenly the water opens out opposite that perfect little square with the white Church in the centre – it was late, and one of us went ashore to see if there was any chance of a meal. He came back uncertain. 'Well, I don't know. I found quite a nice taverna, but I wasn't getting anywhere with the Patron, then an old man came along who was more helpful and I think he's promised me something. He kept tapping his watch, and I kept holding up my fingers to show there were four of us. At least, that's what I meant, but he may have taken it some other way. The only thing that worries me is that I don't think anyone had been eating there tonight. There were just the usual few sitting drinking coffee, or just sitting.' It didn't seem promising, and as everyone was hungry I cooked a meal, I forget what, probably a pasta or risotto as they're quick. Then we went ashore to explore the town and have a drink, and in case the old man really was expecting us, we went first to the taverna. And there he was, peering round the door, getting worried. He hurried us to a laid table, and produced two lovely dentici. But we had just eaten! We couldn't disappoint him, he had been round the corner to the closed fish market, knocked them up, chosen the fish, brought it back and cooked it. How awful if we hadn't gone back! For ever after, this was our restaurant in Gayo.

At Parga we ate rather badly at a restaurant on a rickety platform built out over the sea. Afterwards, when we were picking our way over the beach in the dark back to our dinghy, we nearly fell over some travelling carpet-sellers who had come there to spend the night, and were already asleep. Each had rolled himself tightly into one of his mats, and as these were fairly stiff they could not bend their knees or release their arms, so they looked rather like mummies. We stepped very carefully between them for fear of flicking a pebble into their faces. The next night we saw two priests eating at another restaurant in the town, their neat buns of grey hair put up with hairpins. They are good people to follow, and we ate better there. Next door was a shoe shop, so close that I could reach out from where I sat at our table to choose slippers and try them on over the apéritif. I bought soft black felt ones embroidered in gold.

Naxos is the only working, commercial port we sailed into,

and a group of men on the quay stared at us with such fixed, impassive faces (they all looked like pirates) that we wondered if for the first time in Greek waters an English boat was unwelcome, and it would be unwise for us all to go ashore together leaving *Mary Deare* unattended. It was, after all, the height of the Cyprus troubles. We decided to risk it, and after mooring beside a caique loaded with potatoes – not nearer than we could help, as both rats and cockroaches are good jumpers – we all went ashore, saying '*Kalispera*' hopefully. The most menacing of the group got to his feet and said ponderously but very distinctly, 'Wel-comb to Naxos.'

We walked to the end of the quay and back looking for somewhere to eat. There were three restaurants; all looked small, dingy and depressing. But outside the smallest, an old man with a very sweet smile was grilling fresh mackerel over a charcoal brazier and sprinkling them with almonds, so we went in. The men eating there were stevedores; there was one empty table, and enough chairs, though they were a bit rickety. The old man spread a clean cloth, brought, even there, the knives and forks wrapped in a paper serviette and the freshly-rinsed glasses. We had the usual cucumber and tomato salad, strong but drinkable retsina, fresh bread, and the delicious mackerel with almonds. Once again, a meal no great chef would despise, because the simple ingredients were all good of their kind, fresh and well cooked. This meal on Naxos cost us the equivalent of two-and-six a head.

On Meganisi we liked to anchor in the bay at Port Atheni, where the women come down the hill with baskets of washing on their heads and wash it at the edge of the limpid water, while the black donkeys who have brought down the biggest loads wait under the olive trees. We used to climb the rocky path beside a myrtle hedge smothered in white flower, up to the straggling, terraced village of Vathahort, where visitors are such an unusual diversion that a growing train of curious, friendly people fell in behind us as we explored. On Sundays – but only on Sundays – a little boy grills skewers of meat over a tray of coals which he fans into flame with a spray of leaves, plucking a new one from the tree above him when the one he is using singes away, and sprinkling the skewers with origano and rough salt. For some reason they are the most delicate and delicious skewers any of us had ever tasted. He stands at the side of the kafeníon, and we watch and smell as we sit on the terrace looking down over the steep village.

In Vathahort, too (but again only on Sundays), many of the girls wear dresses with the wicker-stiffened supporting bodices of the ancient bare-breasted Cretan fashion, but with a blouse underneath and generally a brooch at the high neck. Other girls wear modern, short nylon dresses from the mainland shops. Had there been battles over this at home, I wondered?

That was in 1965. We sailed past Meganisi again a few years later, but it wasn't Sunday, we were pressed for time, we didn't put into Port Atheni. I dare not go back there, or to any of these places, for fear they would be different.

Greece for us began and ended with Pylos. It was our first port of entry, and we cleared the ship's papers there at the end of our last season in Greek waters. I had my first *mezo* and retsina on the edge of the quay looking out over vast Navarino Bay, below whose waters the Turkish fleet still lies where Admiral Codrington sunk them. And over the hill is the site of Wise Nestor's house, where Telemachus came searching for news of his father Odysseus.

Our last day in Greece we lunched for the first time at our usual kafeníon – we had always been there in the evening before – and so when I went into the kitchen to say goodbye to our hostess, I found her stuffing the peppers I had so often eaten later in the day. She was chopping up the onions and tomatoes with great speed but very thoroughly, then mixing

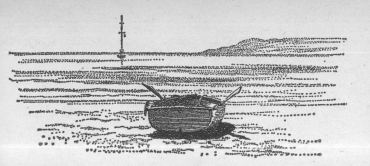

them with *un*-cooked rice, and stuffing the neatly uniform cup-shaped green peppers. This was a discovery, because the recipes say cooked rice. But the juice of the tomatoes, and the very lavish sprinkling of olive oil, provide enough liquid to cook the rice, which becomes soft but not mushy. She allowed an hour in what I would judge a moderate oven.

How lovely they look, those great trays of shining green peppers and bright red tomatoes, packed in tight rows to hold each other up! I have often seen them brought to the bakery – yes, the bakery – of a small town to be cooked in their big ovens, and collected later in the day.

On the afternoon of this last day, we climbed to the castle above Pylos, because we had so often sailed in on this land-mark, but never visited it. An old Venetian fort, empty and abandoned, a ruin, but the barracks and prison cells had been recently used, we thought. Of all the evil-haunted places I have ever been in, I can remember none which one so urgently hurried to leave. It was alive and creeping with horror, that circle of cells on the short grass above the beautiful bay; it shouted at you. It reached out after you.

We hurried back to the town and found it seething with people, gay and celebrating. The quay, usually bare, was packed with tables. We discovered they were celebrating the equivalent of our Navy Day. There were swimming races, sailing races, and then as the quick dark fell, flares were lit all round the huge historic shore, and finally a mass of small boats raced in from every direction, having on their decks canisters of fire. You couldn't see the boats, only clouds of flame and smoke, simulating ancient battles. Our last Greek night.

We made our entry into Turkey at Bodrum, once the Greek

city Halicarnassus, where Mausolus built his enormous tomb
and gave us the word Mausoleum. We discovered fish-kebab,
delicious skewers of fish, in a small restaurant on the edge of
the town, in one of a row of modern houses that might have
been a suburb anywhere, then climbed a hill up to the old
Greek theatre, and were looking for some ancient Greek
sepulchres when on the other side of a bush we met a camel
grazing. I had never before seen camels so far from humans,
untethered; several of them turned loose to roam the hillside
and find their supper. How do they ever catch them again?
I suppose they come to the call.

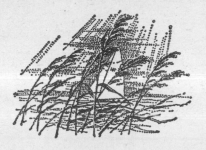

I don't think I can believe that I shall never sit at this table again – serve at this table again. I always sat at the corner nearest to the galley, so I could slip in and out to serve easily.

I remember the first meal on board, the first morning out on *Mary Deare*'s maiden voyage from the Deben Estuary, where she was launched, to the Limfjord in the north of Denmark. For almost the only time, I was feeling rather ill in spite of my Avomine (nerves because everything was so new, and being put to the test after months of plans and preparations? – the first night in my new bunk in the short, choppy movement of the North Sea?). I thought everyone must feel as I did, fragile, and when I said 'What would you like for breakfast?' I rather hoped for a tentative request for black coffee and toast. But 'What we had yesterday would be hard to beat,' said the last Watch enthusiastically, divesting himself of his oilskins. I couldn't believe it – yesterday we'd still been in the Deben, waiting for our engine trials, compass adjustment, sailmakers. How could anyone consider that sort of breakfast today? How could I possibly . . . ? Stunned, I went to the galley. I don't remember who spread the gay new cloth on the table, and distributed my shining new multi-coloured Melaware, and the Scandinavian stainless steel knives and forks. Laying the table was as easy as we had planned, by anyone sitting in the saloon, because the galley lockers have double sliding doors on both sides. Well, this was what they were all for, no good not to use everything I'd carefully planned. I served the lot: grapefruit, cereal, eggs and bacon, bread and Cooper's Oxford marmalade, coffee. Two servings, I always ate last with the Helmsman. This became *Mary Deare's* classic breakfast, until we were in the Mediterranean five seasons later, and then honey took the place of marmalade, and it might be melon or wood straw-berries instead of tinned grapefruit, and no one wanted a hot breakfast. Except after a night sail – then it was always bacon and eggs, even gliding across the Gulf of Lyons in a pellucid dawn, or slipping past Cape Matapan on the brief morning breeze.

There was something wonderful about these breakfasts after a night sail. The men shared the night watches, and I was often called about 6.0 for the dawn watch. It was worth hurry-ing to see the sun break the rim of the horizon – redly. Only a few minutes later it would be climbing up the sky, already gold. It was always worth catching the wild swift-changing colours of sunrise and sunset, with the moon palely balancing the other side of the sky. I would stay at the helm till they woke, and breakfast was leisurely and violently talkative, while the day established itself over the sea, and *Mary Deare* moved forward under the great white peak of her sails.

Lunch was cold, except perhaps for soup in heavy weather, salad lunches with fish, meat, cheese. Oh, the cheeses of Normandy and Brittany, and the great market in Douarnenez! Do the country girls still stand in a row, so prim and pretty, each behind the group of produce she herself has brought to town? Eggs from her hens, the butter she has churned, the cream cheeses she has made?

I've sliced tomatoes with my special knife ('Can't think how they're allowed to make anything so dangerous') from Norway to Turkey. A constant thing, the tomato, all round Europe. The greenstuff disappears at both ends of the Continent – rare in Scandinavia outside the few big ports, very rare in the Eastern Mediterranean. I did buy Cos lettuces in the Dodeca-nese island of Cos from which they are reputed to have come, but they were very coarse. In Cagliari at the bottom of Sardinia I found, miraculously, long fresh-looking Cos lettuces correctly tied with bass. When I opened them at sea, after we'd sailed, I found all the heart had been cut out, and the outer leaves folded together again. In Crete, at the far end of the market at Heraklion, I bought bunches of a kind of watercress, quite different from ours, but green and fresh and tangy, only it didn't last. Often in Greece, at the bigger ports, I found bunches of the herb they insist is parsley, so big-leaved it makes a good salad, but that, too, goes slimy the second day. So when the richness that begins with Denmark and ends with France – in my sea-marketing experience, between Aalberg and St Tropez – is left behind, it's the Serbian salad of thinly-sliced tomatoes, with onions and green peppers, or tomatoes with cucumbers; or courgettes, delicious raw or lightly cooked and served cold with a vinaigrette. Or, if too long at sea, and among ports too small to have anything fresh, one can make a cheat-salad of tinned butter beans with anchovies and black olives; or packet green peas cooked and cold with tinned mushrooms and hard-boiled egg. Tinned celery hearts are good cold, too. The salad dressing is fun when the olive oil bottle has been re-filled from the home-made olive press behind a man's cottage, bought under the tree they grew on, and the vinegar bottle filled from the cask in the local taverna.

Dinner could be a lovely meal on board, forever associated to me with certain times of day and colours of the sea and sky. When that steely look begins to creep over the water, and people ask for sweaters to be thrown up on deck, when the circle of the horizon hardens, then I know it must be time to go below and see about a meal. Someone serves drinks, and mine is safely wedged in a corner beside the radio.

The difference between land and sea is that the sea moves. This is all you need to know about sea-cooking. The rest is just recipe-stuff, which anybody can adapt for themselves from the endless cooking books. You find by experience the best (safest and easiest to get at) locker for each group of stores, in relation to how often you use the different things. *Mary Deare*'s galley is designed with more practical imagination for convenient use in all circumstances than any galley I have yet seen in a small sailing ship, and I'm honoured the Chichesters wanted to use as much as possible of the design in their new boat, then being discussed with Robert Clarke. Cooking pots never rattle in my deep saucepan locker. Butter and cheese and bacon keep firm and fresh in hot seas in my 'cold' locker against the steel hull below the water line. Vast piles of stores, groceries, greengroceries, potatoes, bread, stacked on the quay at the beginning of a season, disappear without trace into her galley lockers. A very comprehensive cellar goes into her bilge-lockers. And she is a racer-cruiser; all this is incidental to her performance at sea.

My cooking on board is *at sea*. I never cook in port. Why sail to a place unless you want to explore it? – and what better way than to eat and drink in its restaurants and cafés, and shop in its markets? You are not a tourist, but an honorary citizen when you are shopping for essential food.

I never served the same dinner twice in a week, indeed, I tried never to give anyone the same main course twice, and we generally invited friends to crew with us for about a fortnight, which meant four ship's companies in a two months' cruise.

What did we eat? Wonderful fresh fish round the cooler coasts, grilled with butter and lemon. Occasionally we caught fish ourselves, if we were going slow enough to have a line over the stern – usually mackerel, which we discovered by experiment to be best cooked in the pressure cooker. Just caught it is too strong, in the sense of being hard and muscular, to fry or grill well. The secret is not to leave it a second too long, else it would begin to break up; the first delicious whiff of cooked fish, and the pressure cooker must be taken off and put under the cold tap (the sea water tap will do, no point in wasting the fresh water). Once, leaving La Rochelle, I asked our favourite restaurant there to cook us a chicken in cream and brandy to take to sea. We ran into a gale, and I was tormented by fear the chicken would go bad before conditions became suitable for such a meal. The patron had given it to me in a brown casserole of his own, with a little triangle broken out of its rim to form a spout. 'For your ship,' he said, 'you can cook in it on board.' The storm passed just in time, and the third evening out we ate our splendid dish, with a worthy bottle of wine, and a good selection of French cheeses to follow, while *Mary Deare* ran smoothly but very fast under glittering stars, with only a small shred of sail up, towards the NW corner of Spain. I remember once in Norway we bought a whole salmon, because by the time we'd measured off the amount we needed, to have it hot one day and with mayonnaise the next, it didn't seem worth leaving the rest. And once in little Port Souzon on Belle Ile in the Bay of Biscay, a particularly elegant member of our crew ate his dinner with

a bloody newspaper parcel under his chair – fresh sardines off the fishing boat just in when we landed for dinner, too special a delicacy not to make sure of.

Except for the first night or so after leaving a port, dinner at sea meant dinner out of stores – a curry of tinned crab and hard-boiled eggs, spaghetti with a sauce invented by a Maltese friend when he crewed with us, made from tinned beef with tomatoes and onions and anchovy fillets; tinned ham sliced and grilled with pineapple slices. Risotto with tunny, tagliatelle with prawns, tongue with sherry sauce, mushroom omelette. And in the Mediterranean, often stuffed peppers or aubergines, or a ratatouille. In Ponza we used to buy *mozzarella*, the buffalo cheese of Southern Italy. It is not so generally found now there are fewer buffaloes, and makes a wonderful welsh rarebit served with bacon on top.

I was always kept informed of sunset and moonrise while I was cooking, so I didn't miss anything wonderful. In Greek or Italian or Turkish waters, after the middle of June, it was very hot in the galley with the cooker's heat added to the accumulated heat of the day (though much less so than it would have been in a wooden hull) and it was life-saving to go up the hatch for a moment into the cool evening, and see some breathtaking phantasmagora of red and gold and purple over wild coasts or a shining empty sea. The land takes on a grape-like bloom as the light drains away. I would serve the first three people, then take my drink and sit in one of the little seats so perfectly positioned between the deck and the saloon. Looking up, I saw the silhouette of the helmsman blur as it grew darker, and stars came out behind his head. Looking down, I saw the lit table, gay with candles and wine and flowers, the animated faces round it – such a long sequence of different faces over the years.

Such a sequence of wines, too, from the great names on the French bottles (those given to us by friends in the Bordelais

lasted for several seasons after we sailed up the Gironde to visit them), to the bottles – any bottles with a good closure, from Dom to Lime juice – which we took to the Greek wine shops and, tasting our way round the casks, had filled up with the retsina we liked best. In Gayo on Paxos I remember, we bought the local wine by weight in the general store. They weighed each bottle empty, then filled it and weighed again. Marsvin and Farmers from Malta; Gozo wine; Campidano Red or White in Sardinia, or Sardinian Gold, a Vermouth. Moscato from Syracuse, Zucco of Palerma. The sweetish Muscatel wines of Calabria or Pantelleria; Samos wine; strangely labelled Turkish bottles. Each wine so right for its own climate and food.

After dinner I went on deck while the others washed up. The two worlds divide so sharply – the warm lit domestic scene below, the talk and laughter in the galley (people always talk so much on *Mary Deare*, even people who are quiet at home), and on deck the cool empty night, the extraordinary loneliness of a small ship making her way across the vast expanse of sea. I go forward, quite a long walk, it seems, past the coach-roofing, the rigging, the mast, the forward hatch, up into the bows. Here one is conscious of the life and effort of the ship herself, ceaselessly stepping over the endless waves. Holding the forward rigging I can lean right over. Her bow line is beautiful, and she throws a very pretty bow-wave. The rhythm of the water flung back by her progress is mesmeric, always one must wait for the next. Often there is phosphorus shining in the water she flings back. One night, and one night only in all the years, the phosphorus formed stars. The whole foaming white cascade was spattered with perfect silver stars. I felt each gush must be the last – it couldn't happen again, but it did, it went on and on, fairylike, magic.

Sometimes at night I have sat for hours on the forward hatch, under the great white curve of the genoa, passing the placid low shores of Denmark, or the wild Calabrian coast with tumbled rocks filling its dry river beds and the towering peak of Etna blocking out a triangle of stars. Even the helmsman at the other end of the ship, the binnacle light catching his yellow oilskins, is far away. Only the ship herself is alive and present, making the effort of her progress, her strong capable advance across the curve of the earth, the age-old power of the wind in the sail.

Of course it isn't always like that. Sooner or later on every voyage, there comes the nightmare spell of bad weather, when to move about the ship at all is a strenuous and calculated exercise, moving carefully from handgrip to handgrip, taking care not to be thrown – always one hand for the ship and one for yourself. Then I am a sea-mouse, trying to keep life as comfortable as possible below decks, ensuring food and rest. I have never wanted to be the one who puts on a safety harness over oilskins and crawls forward to change sail in force eight and upwards. There were always men to do it better. But I learned in my first gale that the only thing to be afraid of in a good ship well sailed, is that people become too tired – especially the most experienced men, because they will be thinking forward to the next thing instead of concentrating on what they're doing, will do most, will use more mental energy thinking what else, if anything, it might be advisable to do to assist the ship; especially, for all these reasons plus total responsibility, the skipper. So, ever since I instinctively got out of my bunk and went to the galley in that first gale between Dinard and Peter Port (on our first sea-going boat, *Triune of Troy*), I have felt the urgent necessity to give each man whatever he can eat, at every change of watch. Hot soup or stew and cheese sandwiches seem to go down best – coffee, Marmite, beef tea. At these times my world closes down to the area of the galley, every inch of it essential and used.

(The carefully planned space between taps and wall just holds milk bottles, mugs, tins, safe on either tack, in any movement; everything must be wedged in some place if you are leaving it out for a second. One finds a safe place for everything, or else puts it back; it is all meticulously plotted, like a game of chess, the right place, the right order. Never for a moment must anything be put down outside the little inviolate area of the galley, for fear it might imperil somebody's quick dash from deck to chart table – or merely slip about and make a mess.)

On my wonderful wooden bar, which slots across the galley when there is much movement on the ship, I can sit astride with my ankles locked and have both hands free. The gas cooker (two rings and a grill) swings level in its gimbals, and has never failed me. Only once I forgot the principle of the gimbals – a night sailing east from Gibraltar. We had had an extremely violent electrical storm our last night at the Rock, and the Met. Office warned us there would be a heavy swell, but as we'd already lost time we decided to leave. There was no wind to fill a sail, so we had to motor. The swell, combin-

ing (if that is the word) with the strong current through Gibraltar Straits, gave us the most uncomfortable night I have ever known. The ship was thrown about in the unpredictable way usually only experienced if you get caught in a race, which made the simplest operation difficult. Two of our company, who had only just joined us, were not surprisingly flat in their bunks, when the fifth member, Ian Peradon (of all her crews the man to whom perhaps *Mary Deare* owes most), came down looking dazed with blood dripping from – I thought – his eye. He had been up forward helping Ralph, who was setting a small sail to steady the motion a little, and had been flung against a mast winch. I dressed it as well as I could (thank God it had just missed the eye), and made him sit down with a whisky. At the end of the voyage he had only a tiny white scar left. I went back to the galley thinking, 'I'm not sailing a ship, I'm running a sick-bay,' and groped stupidly for a spoon that had slipped under the stove; of course my hand checked the swing of the gimbals and the momentary jerk made a drop of boiling soup fly out of the saucepan into my eye. So for the rest of that evening I had one eye and was weeping copiously from the other.

I never looked out when the seas were big (except when we were light crewed and I had to take the helm while Ralph navigated, and then I daren't look over my shoulder at the waves swelling up). My little domestic world below seemed too improbable in the midst of that huge wild water. But there was a curious fascination, especially at night, in this contrast, when I was below and suddenly the hatch was pushed back and someone came down and slammed the hatch to again and struggled out of streaming oilskins and neck scarf, and going to the chart table switched on the light above it to check our course and fill in the log, and for a moment the two worlds joined.

All these memories and many more were behind me like a tide as we jumped out of our hired car on Malta Marina, the last day of our last season. Somewhere safely locked in memory was the night fireflies came out to us like sparks over the sea as we lay in port at Vasilico on Levkas. That night there were nightingales as well as cicadas and the croaking of frogs. Somewhere, too, the only occasion on which I ever actually caught the wind rising. I woke, in harbour, at Sami in the Ionian, everything absolutely quiet and still; then, very far away, a stir so faint one doubted it. Then it came nearer, growing all the time, just like a giant striding towards us, until at last it reached us, and the halyards began to flap against the mast, and then the boat moved restlessly, disturbed even in the sanctuary of harbour. And I lay on my bunk in the dark and knew that sooner or later we must go out to face it, reefed down, in oilskins, wary, prepared.

And all the long, hot blue days, lying on deck in the shade of the sails, while the grey-green islands slid past. All the times the cry of 'Dolphins' had been raised, the black fins cutting the water, advancing in a rolling line, then playing and leaping close against our bows – once one deliberately splashing water with his tail up to a camera held out between the guardrails.

I think we feared the last visit, because we left the car engine running and both doors open as if to say we couldn't stay long.

Just ten years since I had launched her. I had said, 'I name you *Mary Deare*. May you carry us and our friends safely and happily to many far places.'

Now she was stripped out ready to be laid-up as usual in Manoel Island yard – all that was different was that we should not be coming back next year, or ever. I feared some appalling sense of abandonment and betrayal would envelop me when I went on board.

Her boom was bare of mainsail, which always makes a sailing ship look mutilated. Below, we had left her bare, everything had gone into store – the pale gold Dunlopinos gone, leaving the rubber straps; her big multi-coloured cushions, all the galley equipment; all her 'bits', given her in different countries by different people who had sailed in her (the copper measuring jugs from the Aegean, the tin olive oil can from the Ionian, the walnut candlesticks from Majorca, the great

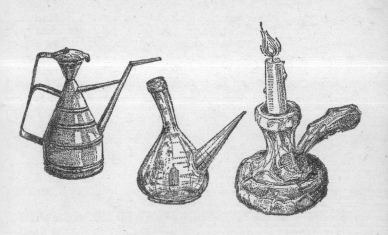

patterned plate from Ibiza, the water bottles from Gibraltar, the cigarette box from La Rochelle, the fruit basket from Douarnenez, ash trays from Norway, from Kiel). The wall was bare of the small maps recording each of her voyages, which were her battle honours; no clock, no barometer. No charts on the chart table. Nobody's clothes in the wardrobe.

But when I unlocked the door and pushed back the hatch and went down into her for the last time, the atmosphere that met me was very different from what I had expected. Certainly there was an atmosphere, it was not negative. But it was surprisingly independent, strong, alert.

Standing in the empty familiar place which had been a part of my life, I realized it was not we who were leaving her, but she who was leaving us. In the life-span of ships she was still young. She was only waiting till somebody else turned her head again to the harbour mouth. The ships we build will sail the sea long after we are dead.

Woodbridge Tide Mill, Suffolk, where
Mary Deare *was launched*

Dorothy Hammond Innes is the wife of Hammond Innes the author, and has shared much of his travel. She has not written a book before, but she has written plays, three of which have been professionally performed, under her maiden name Dorothy Lang. She was an actress before her marriage, and was born in Shanghai.

Fontana Books

Fontana is best known as one of the leading paperback publishers of popular fiction and non-fiction. It also includes an outstanding, and expanding, section of books on history, natural history, religion and social sciences.

Most of the fiction authors need no introduction. They include Agatha Christie, Hammond Innes, Alistair MacLean, Catherine Gaskin, Victoria Holt and Lucy Walker. Desmond Bagley and Maureen Peters are among the relative newcomers.

The non-fiction list features a superb collection of animal books by such favourites as Gerald Durrell and Joy Adamson.

All Fontana books are available at your bookshop or newsagent; or can be ordered direct. Just fill in the form below and list the titles you want.

- -

FONTANA BOOKS, Cash Sales Department, P.O. Box 4, Godalming, Surrey, GU7 1JY. Please send purchase price plus 7p postage per book by cheque, postal or money order. No currency.

NAME (Block letters)

_____

ADDRESS

_____

_____

_____